Opening the Borders

Solving the Mexico/U.S. Immigration Problem For Our Sake and Mexico's

By Larry Blasko

Level 4 Press, Inc.

Dedication

This book is dedicated to all immigrants to America, past, present and future. God bless you all and God Bless The United States of America!

The author of this book is solely responsible for the accuracy of all facts and statements contained in the book.

Copyright © 2007 by Level 4 Press, Inc.

All rights reserved, including the right to reproduce this book, or portions thereof, in any form.

This book is printed on acid-free paper.

Published by
Level 4 Press, Inc.
13518 Jamul Drive
Jamul, CA 91935
www.level4press.com

BISAC Subject Heading: SOC007000   SOCIAL SCIENCE / Emigration & Immigration
Library of Congress Control Number: 2006937615

Preface

Ronald Reagan saw that
   "shining city upon a hill."
Lady Liberty awaits
   "... the homeless, tempest-tost to me,
   I lift my lamp
   beside the golden door!"

But the rest of us don't see much shining light because we flip the Ostrich bit when we spy someone who doesn't speak our English, dress in our clothes, eat our food, or pray where and how we pray.

Immigration—and the opposition to it—has been a recurring theme of American life since at least the Alien and Sedition Acts of 1798, and if you count the understandable distaste of native Americans for the gun-toting folks who showed up uninvited, long before that.

Over the course of our last couple of centuries, we have feared, hated or at least been made very uncomfortable by immigrants like these:

- Catholics. In the first half of the 1800s, the immigrants were mostly Roman Catholic, particularly the Irish, although there were others. This wasn't unexpected—much of Europe was Catholic. But that made the immigrant different and that slid into concerns that the immigrants were taking jobs away from the natives, bringing crime and "immoral practices" (customs different from our own) and who knows what other ills. Some knew nothing at all, and the pro-native American Party, aka "Know-Nothings" would be a major political force by the mid 1850s.

- Chinese. They came to the West, worked hard and long, looked different and talked funny. Well, there you have it—another group taking jobs away from natives and wallowing in their foreign ways. First they were bottled, whether by choice or pressure, in "Chinatowns," then bedeviled by Congress in the Chinese Exclusion Act of 1882.

- People Who Talk Funny. Well, the Irish and English spoke American, sort of, but the Poles, Germans, Italians, Hungarians, Russians and the rest insisted on speaking Polish, German. Italian, Hungarian, Russian and other tongues to each other, not to mention Jews from any of those countries who might also speak Yiddish or Hebrew. A crisis! At the turn of the century, the call was to "Americanize" these folk for their own good. This particular bit of nonsense lives on in today's English-Only movement.

Now the Cause for Alarm is the 12 million or so illegal aliens in the United States, something like 85 percent of them from Mexico. The figures are necessarily imprecise—being illegal, they aren't exactly forming lines to help the census.

Twelve million is a big number, and those immigrants form significant percentages of the labor in agriculture, construction and service industries, whether on the books or off. They're here for the old and familiar reasons that President Reagan and Lady Liberty would understand in a heartbeat—they want better lives for themselves and their families and are willing to risk much and work hard to get them.

That sparks old and familiar charges against them—they're taking native jobs, they don't speak English and they have their own customs.

The response is old and familiar, too. Cries of moral outrage from the House and Senate advocate everything from mass deportation to amnesty. Of course, the niggling details of just how you might deport 12 million souls are details best left to Staff.

(Note To Staff: If you want to accomplish the task in a year, that works out to deporting almost 23 illegal aliens every minute, which is going to cut into your social life—not to mention the time you have to spend on the Congressman's yard because you just deported his lawn service.)

The time-honored and very necessary sport of Congress-bashing aside, our wave of illegal immigrants from Mexico is an enormous opportunity wrapped in the skin of an enormous problem. Our task as Americans is to peel away that skin so we all—Mexicans and Americans alike—can enjoy the fruit of opportunity.

While it's an admittedly risky approach to political discourse, this book is going to examine how we got where we are, how that looks, where we ought to go and how to get there. A similar approach happens in business and family matters daily. It happens in government rarely.

The hope is that this book will spark one of those rare moments.

Larry Blasko
Summit, New Jersey

James K. *Who?*

At least that was what the Whig party crows cawed in the election of 1844, when the Democrats, frustrated after eight futile ballot attempts to nominate former one-term president Martin Van Buren, turned to James K. Polk, who, at best, had been considered for a vice-presidential slot.

This was understandable. Polk had served in Congress representing Tennessee beginning in 1828, and by 1835 had become Speaker of the House of Representatives. Yet he left in 1839 to run for Governor of Tennessee, which he won in a squeaker, but only for one term. His two attempts after that to crawl back into the Statehouse got a "Thanks, but no thanks," from Tennessee voters, and by 1844 he was generally thought to be so politically bankrupt as to be vice- presidential material.

His substantial turn of fortune came from understanding that what we would call "Don't Mess With Texas" might not always be good advice.

All blisters have causes, and this one started when Mexico in the 1820s invited Americans to settle that part of Mexico known as Texas. What harm to let a few gringos settle in lands few Mexicans wanted?

Well, they settled and settled and settled. Along with their pots and pans, they brought their politics and their pro-skeptic American attitude about government, which was something Mexico hadn't expected and certainly didn't want.

They got it anyway, and the Texans, as they began to call themselves, became the too-tight shoe of Mexico. For a few years, the blister grew and festered.

Finally, it popped.

Bridling at what they saw as the caprice—and occasional brutality—of the kaleidoscopic turn of Mexican governments and politics, Texans revolted. Whether it was the stirring call for freedom—"Remember the Alamo!"—or a nakedly opportunistic land grab enabled by Mexican political turmoil, the Republic of Texas was established as an independent nation in 1836.

Texas politicians promptly turned north and began a Salome-Seven-Veils dance of cross-border seduction that would lead to the US annexation of the Republic Texas in 1844, a move that was one of the root causes for more than 20 years of turmoil to follow, most of it bloody, all of it wrapped in westward expansion and slavery. Domestically, with the issue of slavery already at the boiling point, a fragile balance had been maintained in the Senate, with 13 slave states and 13 free states, the result of the Missouri Compromise that has admitted free-state Maine in 1820 and slave-state Missouri in 1821.

The balance was seen by most as crucial to maintaining a union already under stress from both the moral and underlying economic divides that were part of slavery's enormous baggage.

So, the balance would continue with slave-state Arkansas in 1836, balanced by Michigan in 1837. An evenly divided United States Senate provided a legislative body living, yet paralyzed and so in no way dangerous to the status quo.

This was exactly what was wanted, most thought, and then the Texans came galloping to the door, busting up the party.

Admitting Texas would add another slave state to the scales. And since Mexico, when someone was in charge, still considered Texas a rebellious province, it might lead to a war. On the other hand, Texas was an obviously rich prize.

With a presidential campaign afoot, Texas was a thorny problem begging for resolute leadership. The duty fell to the two leading pre-convention presidential candidates, Democrat Van Buren and Senator Henry Clay of Kentucky, the Whig front-runner.

The two politicians did indeed provide resolute leadership on the Texas

4

question. They resolved to take it out of the campaign, both Whig and Democrat voicing public opposition to annexation. Whether or not they were in fact opposed, or merely playing political tiddly-winks, isn't clear.

What is clear is that Polk took an unequivocal stance to annex Texas, and threw in a bold stance on the Oregon territories disputed with Britain since 1818. Both were positions more popular in the saloons than the salons of the time, but as Polk's patron, Andrew Jackson had proved democracy wasn't confined to the elite. Jackson had worked with success to remove property and class qualifications for voting, and the voting population after 1828 included more or less all adult white males. That changed politics in that appealing to the masses now had a tremendous impact.

Polk's move, whether or not by conviction, would have been applauded by today's marketers, who strive for what makes their product *different*.

The Democrat's platform strongly backed their nominee's view on Texas and Oregon, as did President Tyler. But since a ninth-ballot nomination is hardly selection by acclamation, Polk faced an uphill battle.

The electoral vote was 170 for Polk and 105 for Clay, but the popular vote difference was less than 40,000. We're not talking mandate here.

For Texas, it turned out not to matter. Congress whipped out a joint resolution authorizing the annexation of Texas and President Tyler signed it on March 1, 1845, three days before Polk took the oath of office.

Unsurprisingly, those in charge of Mexico at the moment cancelled diplomatic relations.

That was the bubbling stew that confronted President Polk as he took office in the spring of 1845.

President Polk, well aware that about as many of his countrymen wanted him out as had wanted him in, could have been a timid caretaker. Instead, he outlined four goals for his administration:

6

1. Reduce the import tariffs; (NAFTA anyone?)
2. Create an independent Treasury (the proto-Fed)
3. Settle the Oregon boundary mess.
4. Get California.

The first and second were internal matters and quickly accomplished. The third, Oregon, had been simmering for years, and Great Britain was the opponent. It had not yet been 40 years since British troops burned the Capitol and looted the White House, so Britain was not to be taken lightly. And, finally, acquiring California conveniently ignored that it had already been acquired, first by Spain and then by Mexico. Its colonial roots went back about a century before Jamestown, and the native Olmec civilization was building cities and temples two thousand years BC, when the *conquistadors* from Spain were lucky to be building huts.

Fate, which had already elevated an unlikely candidate to the presidency, continued to deal President Polk sweet hands. One of the disputes between Mexico and Texas, republic or state, was where the border was. Mexico said it was on the Nueces River. Texas said it was south, on the Rio Grande.

Polk appointed John Slidell as minister plenipotentiary to Mexico to resolve this issue as well as seek the purchase of lands that are now California and New Mexico. Slidell's problem was not the scope of his authority but the merry-go-round of Mexican governments with which he was supposed to treat. One, which had requested someone with the powers of Slidell's office, soon was followed by another, which ordered Slidell to get out in January of 1846.

That government, under the leadership of Mariano Parades y Arriaga, said there was no border dispute—Texas was a rebellious territory of Mexico, not a state of The United States. And they moved troops into the disputed area, although careful to stay on their side of the border they denied, the Rio Grande.

President Polk ordered Zachary Taylor to move troops to the Rio Grande to prevent an invasion of Texas. By March of 1846, Taylor, who later would himself serve as president, was there in modest force with 3,000 troops. He was based in Corpus Christi, about 100 miles south of where the meandering Nueces took a northeastern direction.

The Taylor deployment was interesting. Three thousand troops were certainly not enough for any large military action. And if they were there to defend the good citizens of Texas, it should be remembered that the Texans had taken care of their own defense quite handily for almost a decade. Of course, 3,000 troops in or near disputed territory were quite enough to provoke a Mexican response, and they did, on April 24, 1846 when Mexican cavalry shot up an American scouting force, killing eleven soldiers.

Taylor pursued the Mexicans across the Rio Grande into undisputedly Mexican territory and Congress responded

9

with a declaration of war on Mexico, May 13, 1846.

It wasn't going to be a two-front war. While relations with Mexico had deteriorated, the Oregon question with Britain, in which Mexico also had claims, was resolved by compromise—not including Mexico—between Britain and the United States, which was approved by the Senate in June of 1846. California, long sought, declared itself independent in the same month.

President Polk was on a roll.

It wasn't entirely without opposition. A pain-in-the-butt Whig congressman from Illinois introduced a strongly critical resolution in the House, suggesting that the "Spot" where American blood had been shed wasn't in Texas and had never been in Texas. That was December 22, 1847, and the same gadfly, a little more than a year later would throw this barb from the floor of the House:

"As I have before said, he knows not where he is. He is a bewildered, confounded, and miserably perplexed man. God grant he may be able to show, there is not something about his conscious, more painful than all his mental perplexity!"

Gadfly Congressman Lincoln[i]

Dealing with ornery congressmen is part of the White House job description, as Illinois Congressman Abraham Lincoln would learn when he sat in the White House as President Lincoln and conducted a different war.

11

The Mexican war itself was going quite nicely—unless you were Mexican.

Mexico hadn't figured it that way. First, the probable battlefield was a long way from then-American population centers, so American supply lines would be long. Second, the Mexicans held a 4-1 (at least) numerical advantage.

But between the U.S. declaration of war in June and the following December, Mexico would be wracked by political turmoil, having as head of government in that short time three persons before Antonio López de Santa Ana returned (with U.S. blessing) from exile in Cuba and resumed power. It was a Polk mistake. Others would follow.

Militarily, the U.S. forces were unstoppable. In February of 1847, Taylor's 5,000 troops routed 20,000 Mexicans at Buena Vista. By March, General Winfield Scott would be the proprietor of Vera Cruz and move from there to run Mexico City by September.

The war in Mexico would be a proving ground for a later—and far bloodier—Civil war for Americans. Jefferson Davis,

Sherman, Grant, Lee, McClellan, Meade, Bragg, Jackson, Longstreet, Burnside and others would earn spurs in those combats. The Mexican war finally cost roughly 13,000 American lives, only 1,700 of which were combat-related. Disease took the rest.

With the surrender of Mexico City, the fighting stopped, but the politics continued. On the Mexican side, Santa Ana stepped down as president. That enabled Manuel de la Pena y Pena, the head of the Supreme Court, to assume the acting presidency and the Treaty of Guadalupe-Hidalgo would be signed on February 2, 1848.

On the face, the treaty was a triumph. The United States got California and New Mexico, the Rio Grande was mutually recognized as the border, and except for the Gadsden purchase in 1853, the boundaries of the United States would be pretty much set until Hawaii and Alaska's stars climbed into that blue field.

It was not, as far as we know, what President Polk wanted. Although he had

13

accomplished all of the four goals he had initially set for his administration, he wanted more, but that would have meant more fighting in what had been a war haunted by criticism, including from former president John Quincy Adams. Henry David Thoreau's stinging essays later called "Civil Disobedience," were all the rage of the intellectual East as Thoreau served some jail time for refusing to pay taxes on account of the war.

While President Polk's exact views aren't available, many think he sided with those, including Sam Houston, who advocated taking all of Mexico. That was a red flag to the abolitionist crowd, which saw the possibility of several more pro-slavery states. Whatever Polk believed, he knew that what you believe and what you can get through Congress are often quite different. Polk sent the Treaty of Guadalupe-Hidalgo to the Senate, which approved it. With a reciprocal approval from Mexico, hostilities were over by May, 1848.

Hostilities over, yes; problems over, no. The basic imbalance between life and wages in an oligarchy and a democracy would haunt relations for another 150 years, and still do today. Although accounted by many as one of our "near-great" presidents, President Polk's failure to take all of Mexico was his largest and final mistake.

President Polk would watch his former General, Zachary Taylor, win the White House and would die, childless, on June 15, 1849 at the age of 53, three months after leaving 1600 Pennsylvania Avenue. His wife, Sarah, would survive him until 1891. Both are buried in Nashville.

The problem President Polk left us is very much unburied, in Nashville and hundreds of cities around the United States.

Border? What Border?

One of the greatest fables of our age is that there is a border between Mexico and the United States.

True, cartographers draw a line 1,951 miles long from San Diego/Tijuana in the West to Matamoros/Tamaulipas and Brownsville, Texas. But they're about the only ones who pay any practical attention to it.

Sure, the Border Patrol does its best with a couple thousand agents. But consider the size of the assignment. If we were to station a federal agent every 60 feet along the border, it would take almost 172,000 of them. And that would cover just the first shift.

We could, of course, hire the entire armed forces of Mexico, but that would leave us about 30,000 bodies short for that first shift. As with many things Mexican, the estimates vary.

Mexico Today[ii]

Well, the obvious solution is to increase the amount of territory each guardian watches. Let's give each of them responsibility for 300 feet. Now we can get by with around 34,000 persons a shift. Three shifts a day is a bit more than 103,000 guardians—which doesn't cover weekends, holidays, sick time, etc.

Not to mention administrators, clerks, and the other common flora and fauna of large human undertakings.

And above all, not to mention that it wouldn't work worth a damn. Unless you happen to be in the Goodyear blimp, try watching an area a football field wide. Turns out you can only watch part of it, and *that* only part of the time –

sneezing, blinking, scratching, day-dreaming will all have their due.

So let's bag the human force and build a wall, one of the silliest of the current crop of silly notions rattling though Congress. Some kind soul should whisper to any Congressman who looks capable of understanding it that the idea has been tried before and didn't work.

Ask the Chinese how effective the Great Wall was as a defense measure. Or talk to the French about the Maginot Line. Or former East Germans about the Berlin Wall.

As a pork barrel project of unimaginable proportions for contractors in the Southwest, a wall has a certain charm.

But they'd probably build it with illegal Mexican labor.

This border we obsess about is the busiest international border in the world for both legal and illegal crossings. Most estimates put the legal traffic at 350 million a year. The illegal traffic is around a million, most of it not two-way.

But as the Pew Hispanic Center noted in May 2006, "Nearly half of all unauthorized migrants now living in the United States entered the country legally through a port of entry such as an airport or a border crossing point where they were subject to inspection by immigration officials…"

They just didn't leave when their visas expired. Or used a border crossing card and never crossed back.

Pew puts the legal entry/illegal stay group number at 4.5 to 6 million. Those who scooted around the immigration inspectors or Border Patrol are estimated at 6 to 7 million.

As Carolyn Lochhead of the San Francisco Chronicle wrote in May of 2006, "Roughly 10 percent of Mexico's population of about 107 million is now living in the United States, estimates show. About 15 percent of Mexico's labor force is working in the United States. One in every seven Mexican workers migrates to the United States."

Mexico itself is tough on illegal immigration. Those from Central and South

American trying to get across Mexico's southern border face felony charges and a government (and Constitution) that is hostile to immigrants, legal or otherwise.

So why doesn't our NAFTA buddy Mexico help make the border a border?

Mexico has her reasons—20 billion of them, actually, which is the dollar amount that Mexicans in the US send home each year. That's about the same as Mexico gets from oil exports. And the border-sieve serves as an important safety valve in a country that preaches democracy and practices oligarchy steeped in corruption so widespread that it is the de facto law of the land. That $20 billion—the Mexicans call it "remittances"— accounts for three percent of Mexico GDP. That seems like a low figure until you understand where it's coming from and where it's going. It's coming from those whose poverty in their homeland was unbearable and it's going to help those they left behind.

That money can't be extracted from such a society without widespread turmoil, which is the last thing the U.S.

needs on its southern border, not to mention the last thing the ruling oligarchy needs in Mexico. It's the pin on the few-rich/many-poor grenade that is Mexican society. Unsurprisingly, Mexican politics have long reflected that.

Besides, the U.S. has a significant interest in Mexicans spending stateside-earned dollars in Mexico. The largest private employer in Mexico is Wal-Mart, which controls 30 percent of the supermarket sales, generating more business than the entire tourism industry. With 633 outlets, Wal-Mart does $ 6 billion in food sales alone.

There is more to this than Wal-Mart. Overall, 88 percent of Mexico's exports wind up in the U.S. We are, for the most part, not talking high-tech. According to the United States Department of Agriculture roughly three-quarters of the 2004 imports from Mexico were "beer, vegetables and fruit." Mexicans make beer of surpassing excellence, and their growing season complements that of the U.S.

The USDA says the exports from the U.S. to Mexico are roughly three quarters grains, oilseeds, meat and related products. Overall, the Federal Reserve Bank of Dallas says 56 percent of Mexico's imports come from Uncle Sam.

The same source says U.S. money accounts for 62 percent of all direct foreign investment in Mexico and the value of U.S.-Mexico trade in 2004, the last year available, had grown to $275.3 billion from $89.5 billion in 1993.

And that's just stuff that's on the books.

Whether on the books or off, the Mexican involvement in the U.S. economy is great. According to the Pew Hispanic Center writing about 2005 figures:

- Twenty-four percent, or one out of four, farm workers were illegal immigrants.
- Seventeen percent in the cleaning industry cleaned without a clean legal slate.
- Fourteen percent in the construction industry got themselves a visa with their feet.

- Twelve percent in the food preparation industry didn't stew over border niceties.

Throwing percentages about has an inherent misleading quality, as in "100 percent of my wives have been blonde." Really? And how many was that?

And because those without documentation are more interested in a paycheck than in percentages, all these figures can be questioned in any specific situation. But, on average, look at it this way:

- If there are four guys weeding that field of spinach, one of them would get antsy if asked for ID.
- Of the six folks who clean the floor of your office building, one has an immigration record less than clean.
- One out of six of the guys building your new addition or putting up those condos first built their own— and bogus—identity.
- The chances are that one out of ten of the cooks in your favorite Ital-

ians restaurant isn't a.) Italian or b.) legal.

All of those jobs are hard work, with relatively low pay. And the harder the work, the higher the concentration of illegals, the Pew Center found.

Installing insulation saves energy— and is hot, dirty and dangerous, the least of the dangers being a perpetual itch as little fibers dig into the skin, never mind those burrowing in the lungs. Pew says 36 percent of all insulation workers are illegal.

Roofing, another hot, hard and dangerous task has a 29 percent illegal worker component, according to Pew. That matched those who install drywall, and was just a couple of points away from the 27 percent of butchers and food processing workers who turn a carcass into the nicely packaged stuff in the supermarket. Think cutting your steak is tough? Try cutting it from a 500-pound slab.

With all the current silliness about increased border patrols and walls, all the chest-beating from all sides of the question, the fact remains that immigrants come seeking work and the American people give it to them. If we did not, they would not come.

Or as Walt Kelly said in his Pogo comic strip, "We have met the enemy ... and he is us."

We tend to forget, fellow humans, that we are the largest untamed breeding population of mammals on the planet. And just like our fellow mammals, we move to where we can find food, shelter and the chance to reproduce, borders and other artificial barriers be damned.

Why They Come

The Spanish and English took fundamentally different approaches to what we now call the native Amerindian populations they found, first when Spain invaded Mexico in 1519 and decades later when the English began to invade the East coast of North America in the early 1600s.

While both groups of colonists used military force and disease against the natives, the Spaniards over the course of the centuries would make more love than war. In most of what would become the United States, the preferred method of contact with the native peoples was killing them. In Mexico, it was impregnating them.

Today's demographics in a modern Mexico of some 107 million souls—the world's largest Spanish-speaking country—bear witness. According to the CIA World Factbook, 60 percent of Mexico's population is Mestizo (Amerindian-Spanish), 30 percent is Amerindian, while Caucasians are just nine percent and "other" one percent.

That has resulted in a de facto oligarchy, in which very few citizens control much of the wealth and the government. In all of Mexico's history, the only president of full indigenous blood would be Benito Juárez, a Zapotec Indian whose native tongue wasn't Spanish. (President Porfirio Díaz' mother was a Mixtec Indian, so he was Mestizo.)

It has also resulted in a society where 40 percent live below the official poverty rate, and where ten percent of the population accounts for more than 35 percent of household income. (The bottom ten percent in income accounts for just 1.6 percent.)

In general, the states of Mexico farther to the South are poorer than those to the North. And the southern state of Chiapas, since the mid-90s, has been more under the control of the rebellious Zapatista Army of National Liberation than the central government.

Benito Juarez. [iii]

Although there have been armed clashes, the policy of the Mexican government for more than a decade has been to ignore the Zapatistas, who have established 32 so-called autonomous cities and are waging a war with public

29

relations and infrastructure building. The government response has been "Yeah—so?"

Although they are a nuisance, the Zapatistas do not seriously threaten the power of the elite. In fact, nothing seriously threatens the power of the elite. Yes, Mexico is a popular democracy under its 1917 constitution. But popular democracy only works when the majority of citizens enjoy its fruits—meaning they eat every day and are not consumed with worry about eating the next day.

That is not now the case in Mexico.

The situation is not a theoretical defect in national law. In theory, Mexico's laws have many of the features familiar to U.S. citizens—Social Security, for example and a Minimum Wage law.

It's that minimum wage law that deserves a closer look as part of the answer to why Mexicans head North in record numbers to work.

In June of 2006, the Department of Labor said the United States minimum wage was $5.15 an hour, although it was quick to point out that some states pay much more than that, in which case the state minimum trumps the federal rate. And every once in a while, Congress feels itchy about the next election and bumps the minimum wage a buck or so.

Mexico sets its minimum wage by three geographic areas, A, B and C, and varies them by occupation. It also sets the rate as a daily wage. So, in 2006, an albañil, or general construction handyman, earned, at the minimum, 70.93 pesos per day in an A area, but 66.77 in a C area.

Or, about $6.45 or $6.07 a day in dollar currency at 11 pesos to the greenback Well, but the cost of living is cheaper in Mexico, right?

Not necessarily. According to a comparative shopping list compiled in 2005 by someone who moved from Los Angeles to Lerdo in Durango state. Rollins (Rolly) Brook put up a web site that among other things, converted his shopping list receipt food prices from pesos to dollars.

For low-fat hamburger, he paid $2.47 a pound. That's the equivalent of 30 minute's labor for someone working at minimum wage in the U.S. It's three hours of labor for our general construction handyman in Mexico. And if you find a construction handyman/laborer working for $5.15 an hour in the U.S., you should go buy a lottery ticket because it is indeed your lucky day.

A study released in January 2006 pegged the median *hourly* wage for immigrant day laborers, the jornaleros who gather on street corners or in parking lots, at $10. The study, entitled "On The Corner: Day Labor In the United States," observed that day laborers have good months and bad months but that "...it is unlikely that their annual earnings will exceed $15,000, keeping them at or below the federal poverty threshold."

True, in the United States, with a per-capita annual GDP (Gross Domestic Product) of $42,000. But not too shabby in Mexico with a per-capita annual GDP of $10,100 USD.

So if you were our Mexican albañil (let's call him Al), that $15,000 US would work out to the equivalent of 2,326 days of work at the minimum Mexican wage, about seven and a half years of six-day work weeks.

Any wonder that our buddy Al is looking to head North *muy pronto*?

The study, based on mid-decade interviews, was done by Abel Valenzuela Jr. of UCLA, Nike Theodore of the University of Illinois at Chicago, Edwin Meléndez of the New School University, and Ana Luz Gonzalez who was a Ph.D. student in urban planning at UCLA. It reveals some fascinating tidbits both about the illegal immigrants who have the knickers of the U.S. Body Politic in a twist, and about the immigrants themselves.

Tidbit One: Remember those horrible business folk that exploit illegal day labor? Turns out, according to the study, that 49 percent of the laborers are primarily employed by homeowners or renters. Must give the homeowners or renters enough free time away from their chores to attend anti-immigration rallies.

Tidbit Two: The laborers aren't hanging on the corner to annoy passers-by with the sounds of Spanish. They're doing it to support their families. The study found 36 percent of them married, another 7 percent living with someone. Sixty three percent of them have kids and 28 percent of those kids were born here and are United States citizens.

Tidbit Three: These folks aren't bump-and-run employees. Sixty-nine percent are hired repeatedly by the same employer. That suggests both employers and employees are happy. Would the employers like cheaper rates? You betcha. Would the workers like higher rate? Duh! Is this market capitalism at work, which is what we're supposed to believe in here? You got that one, Sparky, good for you.

Tidbit Four: These folks ain't lazy. The study shows 74 percent of them seeking work five or more days a week, with a third of them looking on all seven days.

The study also explains that many day laborers may be doing it to supplement a second job. Or are using it as a key to get a steady job.

That steady job may or may not be on the books and may or may not (probably not) offer benefits, but when you're in a long, dark tunnel, even a tiny candle is very, very welcome.

Or, as bank robber Willie Sutton may have said, he robbed banks "because that's where the money is."

And immigrants, legal or not, are coming to the United States from Mexico for the same reason. The money and opportunity to earn it are here. The crushing need is there. Anyone who thinks these two tidal forces won't flow to each other—or worse, that they can be stopped—is either not paying attention or failing to take their meds.

Where They Go,
What They're Like

As Neil Diamond stirringly reminds us in song, "They're coming to America!" but it turns out that they're mostly coming to eight states -- at least those very-predominantly Mexican Hispanics we're naming with the shorthand "illegal immigrants."

Some of those eight states are obvious, being Border States. Others are less so. The eight and the percentage of unauthorized immigrants they hold, according to the Pew Hispanic Center:

- California—24 percent
- Texas—14 percent
- Florida—9 percent
- New York—7 percent

- Arizona -- 5 percent
- Illinois—4 percent
- New Jersey—4 percent
- North Carolina—3 percent

The figures are based on three surveys done in March of each year from 2002 to 2004. Putting those percentages in numbers, according to the same source, it looks like this:

- California—2.4 million
- Texas—1.4 million
- Florida—850,000
- New York—650,000
- Arizona—500,000
- Illinois—400,000
- New Jersey—350,000
- North Carolina—300,000

Taking the usual caveat that estimates of illegal immigrants are estimates of persons not anxious to be counted, that still prompts wonder why this is being ballyhooed as a National Problem when it seems to mostly sit in just eight states.

The answer is because while the majority is in those eight states, many are elsewhere, and although their numbers are small in the big picture, they loom large in the town-by-town picture. Or, as Tip O'Neill, the late Speaker of the House taught us, "All politics is local."

While we all may be citizens of the United States of America, and all are bound someday to be Robert Frost's "Townsman of a stiller town," we mostly deal with the things we can see and understand and touch every day. If you want someone's attention, don't talk global politics, talk sales tax, zoning and school districts. We don't really live globally, we live locally. A case in point:

In May of 2006, the national media discovered Crete, Nebraska. Since it is a town of a shade more than 6,000 in Saline County, this is a significant achievement for the national media and not to be downplayed. After all, Crete, Nebraska is not serviced by either the MTA or the Metro and few local conversations are probably about the front pages of the New York Times or the Washington Post.

What the national media discovered was that Crete is home to Farmland, Inc., a meatpacking plant. To Hispanic immigrants from Mexico and elsewhere, Farmland's offer of a $9 hourly wage looked pretty good. So, according to a local Catholic priest, Rev. Julius Tvrdy, as quoted in an Associated Press article, there are maybe 1,700 of them now, up from just 40 in 1990.

The article suggested that this enormous increase has caused some distress at the local level and even injected itself into statewide politics. See, the immigrants are, well *different.* I mean they speak Spanish and all, plus, the article says, there's even a Spanish mass at Sacred Heart.

Or maybe they're not so different. Crime stats are almost flat, the article says, and the newcomers do shop locally. And if there is a God, informed opinion suggests He speaks Spanish as well as English, and maybe even Italian. So are the immigrants carving up your next dinner in Crete an alien invasion or just folks looking for work, trying to raise their kids and worship in their faith?

You know—doing what America is supposed to be about.

Why these Hispanic, mostly Mexican immigrants are here and what that means is a question that can be repeated in small towns across the country, from Crete, where bright-lights-big-city means Lincoln, Nebraska, to Summit, New Jersey, less than 25 miles from Manhattan. Hispanic immigration, most of it from Mexico, the majority of it illegal, is a fact of life.

In Summit, where the median home price is $726,000 and there aren't any meatpacking plants, there are lawns. Acres and acres of lawns, many owned by folks wealthy enough to not personally interact with grass except to walk on it. And houses to be painted. And driveways to be sealed. And roofs that need fixing and houses to be demolished and rebuilt as McMansions. Much of this is being done by immigrants, of whatever legal status, from Mexico and the rest of Latin America. So the parish bulletin of St. Teresa of Avila Roman Catholic Church in this generally very wealthy town of 21,000 is half English and half Spanish.

But the owners of multi-million dollar houses and the folks who mow, paint and whatever share the same super-markets, parks, swimming pools and streets, for the most part amiably and productively. The big-draw local super-markets have special sections for Mexican foods. And this in a town where it was thunderous news when the current mayor was elected—the first declared Democrat in 100 years to hold the job.

So why, from Crete, Nebraska to Summit, New Jersey and in the eight states where mostly illegal Mexican immigrants live, why isn't the world going to Hell in a handbasket?

That's a question conveniently ignored by the "Deport Them All!" crowd, probably because the available facts won't support that position. Of course, facts and political positions are like op-

42

posite magnetic poles, but in spite of the Laws of Political Nature, it's worth a look at these new immigrants, legal or not.

Will these folks be on welfare?

Hardly. According to the Pew Institute, 92 percent of male adult illegal immigrants age 18-64 work. That compares to 83 percent for native folk. But just 56 percent of illegal immigrant women in the same age category hold jobs as opposed to 73 percent of native-born women. As Pew reports, "The principal reason women do not participate in the labor force is the presence of young children in the family."

So, taking it out of the statistical and into the real, it is difficult to demonize a group after admitting that dad is working his butt off and mom is staying at home to handle the equally arduous task of making a home and taking care of the kids. Norman Rockwell would approve. The "Deport Them All!" crowd should approve too, but politics often demands a bogeyman, and this is the one they're stalking.

Declaring yourself in favor of "hard work and family values" apparently precludes many on the right from seeing those values demonstrated by folks who speak Spanish to each other. Of course, they couldn't see them when the folks were speaking Polish, or German or Japanese, Chinese, Russian or whatever either.

The hope is that someday, the Boulder of Enlightenment will bounce off their skulls and they'll realize that being an American, at root, hasn't been based on Where We're From or Who We Are as much as What We Believe and What We Do.

But so many of them are below the poverty level!

Yes, maybe 40 percent of them are. But what we easily forget is that the United States "poverty line" is a goal that much of the world, including many in Mexico, would like to enjoy. If we stop looking at illegal Mexican immigrants with our eyes and try to look at them with their own, they're mostly lots better off here than they were at home. Re-

member that $20 billion in annual re-
mittances? These "poor" folk are supporting others even poorer.

And it can't be discounted that
unlike other immigrants, legal or not,
who arrived from overseas on boats and
airplanes, these can just walk, a travel
method lots harder—but lots cheaper—
than those offered by travel agents, even
counting the work of the coyotes, the
Mexicans who offer to help with the illegal hike to opportunity. Of course, the
coyotes charge—and sometimes don't
deliver—but the conditions of life for
many in Mexico keep their customers
coming anyway.

So yes, they are poor. And if they get
here, many will still be poor as the U.S.
understands it. But not as most Mexicans understand it.

This is the only place on the globe
where a First World country, the Lone
Superpower Standing, shares a border
of almost 2,000 mostly unguarded miles
with what is s Third World country, at
least for those citizens in the southern
half of Mexico's 31 states. That group is

easy to spot on a map of the 2006 Mexican presidential election. They voted for leftist presidential hopeful Andrés Manuel López Obrador, whose support in the whisker-close election that courts said he lost was in Mexico's southern states and in the barrios of Mexico City, where he was once mayor. Much of the current immigration debate in the United States doesn't seem to understand that division along class lines. Maybe it's because they've forgotten that when you're hungry, it is your stomach that decides your vote, not your head.

The Mexicans who are voting with their feet understand that exactly. Their lives are better here. And the many comfortable Americans with leisure to worry that this is a "bad trend in the long run" should ponder the following from the late William Manchester's masterly "The Glory And The Dream," a narrative American history of the middle of the Twentieth Century:

Writing of a Congressional hearing critical of the emerging New Deal, Manchester said "...as Harry Hopkins tartly observed at a congressional hearing, 'People don't eat in the long run, Senator, they eat every day.'"

Illegal immigrants from Mexico already know that, which probably makes them smarter than most Senators, although we shouldn't damn the immigrants by faint praise.

Well, yes, but these immigrants aren't educated!

And they aren't. Again, the Pew Institute says 56 percent of the illegal immigrants lack the equivalent of a high school diploma, and only another ten percent earn a college degree or beyond. So that's roughly five or six million without high-school skills, and somewhere around a million with a four-year sheepskin. But picking strawberries or putting in a driveway requires a type of education no longer taught by most schools for American citizens.

If the practical purpose of an education is to get ahead, the illegal immigrants are already succeeding on those terms. They are having a better life than the one offered by the land they left, and they are giving their children a shot at a far better future, especially those born on U.S. soil and hence citizens.

Besides, their educational profile matches—in many cases exceeds—those of earlier immigrants, those now secured in citizenship, who are sometimes among the first to snarl at those next in line.

This new wave of immigrants have not been so educated as to wonder how many angels may dance on the head of a pin if they can't first afford to buy the pin. If they work as hard as they have been—and if Americans unite to shove this important issue through the unyielding mud of Congress, then it is possible that the children of immigrants will become so highly educated that they are unable to do anything practical or useful, winning approval of the existing American elites at last.

But they get services and don't pay taxes!

"Not hardly" as John Wayne would say. First, like anyone else, they pay sales taxes of all sorts just as U.S. citizens do. Through rent, they pay property taxes. If they're working for cash on a day-labor basis, they dodge Social Security, Medicare and income tax withholding, but if they manage to produce fake documents or otherwise just get on a payroll, they pay all three, plus state taxes. And since they're not officially here, they can hardly file tax returns to claim the refunds that would surely be due most of them.

The Washington group, Center For Immigration Studies (CIS), observes that "On average, the costs that illegal households impose on federal coffers are less than half that of other households, but their tax payments are only one-fourth that of other households." This was part of a study that explored federal services to illegal aliens versus their tax contributions and concluded that the feds were paying out to illegal immigrants more than they were taking in.

Folks paying little or no taxes and costing the feds more than they're paying isn't a situation unique to immigrants. In fact, it is pretty common, but mostly at the other end of the income scale, which is why the Alternative Minimum Tax was born. (The AMT is the way the feds say "Yeah, your accountant is really clever, but we both know you're loaded so you've got to pay anyway.)

The CIS also tackled the myth that illegal immigrants rush to welfare and other social programs, one of those "everyone knows" truisms available from any barstool. Turns out, the CIS said, that "...receipt of cash assistance programs turns out to be very low, while Medicaid use, though significant, is still less than for other households."

The CIS estimated that "On average, illegal households pay more than $4,200 a year in all forms of federal taxes. Unfortunately, they impose costs of $6,950 per household."

Kinda makes you wonder what those figures would be if the homeowners and renters hiring jornaleros and paying no-questions-asked cash made their acts legal. The bet here is that the feds would at least break even, maybe even make a profit. (The CIS, for the record, bets the other way, saying that legalization, putting everything and everyone on the books, might increase the difference between what this group gives the feds and what the feds dish out.)

Still, they don't assimilate, don't speak English and don't learn our ways!

Gimme a break. Every group of immigrants in this nation's history has faced that same nonsense and met it the same way. Parents and grandparents who come here speak the language they learned as children. They teach it to their children. But for their children, it is a second language to English.

The Pew Hispanic Center with surveys in 2003-2004 addressed the speak-English issue pretty forthrightly. Pew found "The endorsement of the English language, both for immigrants and their children, is strong among all Hispanics regardless of income, party affiliation, fluency in English or how long they have been living in the United States."

Their surveys found that 57 percent of foreign-born immigrants agreed that

"...immigrants have to speak English to say they are part of American society..."

And 96 percent of the foreign born said it was "very important" to teach English to their children.

I am the grandson of four Slovak immigrants. My parents grew up speaking, reading and writing Slovak in the home—and native American English outside of it and to their siblings because both my parents were born here. As a child, I heard the grownups speak Slovak only when they were talking to a very old person, or about things like Santa Claus, shopping and sex.

My wife's parents were both Ukrainians who got here in 1953 courtesy of Adolph Hitler and Joseph Stalin and unimaginable—to us—perils and toils. They spoke Ukrainian in the home. Until she arrived in 1953 as a six-year-old, my wife had never spoken a word of English. She had been born in Germany, her sister in Belgium and only her baby brother in the United States.

So did both of those families hang on to their native cultures? In part, yes—

food, religion, language among family in the home, the important and comforting stuff. As has every other immigrant group. And America is a better nation for it. We have managed –and hopefully will continue to manage—to be a nation of Mom and apple pie, Mutter and strudel, Mama and pirogi, Madre and tortillas, and however you say Mother and whatever your favorite comfort food from childhood might be. To follow that metaphor a bit, let's talk about stew.

One of the most unfortunate metaphors to saddle public discourse has been the "melting pot," as if all who entered were supposed to lose their individual identities in becoming some new alloy that would be called "American." Common sense and history shows that instead of a melting pot, it's a stew pot. Every ethnic group contributes its unique flavor to the gravy that binds us all, but they still retain their identity, just as carrots, potatoes, beef, onions and the rest do when they go into the pot. They each don't become something different, but together they become something better.

The Federal Reserve Bank of Dallas, which for obvious reasons has been doing some heavy thinking about these issues, noted in mid-2004 that "Mass immigration of low-skilled non-English-speaking workers is hardly a new phenomenon."

Ya think?

One of the sad things about much of our current education system is that it produces citizens who view a "historical event" as something that happened last year. So for the Federal Reserve Bank of Dallas to remind us of the massive immigration wave of 1890 to 1920, followed by the post World War II wave is a public service, especially for the "Deport-Them-All" crowd, at least those of them who read.

And here's the part of that Dallas Fed report every "Deport-Them-All" person ought to read daily:

"Interestingly, despite lacking a high-school diploma, low-skilled immigrants still outperform native dropouts in the labor market. Low-skilled male immigrants are more likely to work, as seen in their higher labor-force participation rates, and are less likely to be unemployed.

"Because of the commitment to work— and despite other disadvantages such as lack of English fluency and familiarity with U.S. laws and institutions— immigrants assimilate and surpass earnings levels of like natives after about 16 to 20 years in the United States."

So, if the Dallas Fed is right, these immigrants don't learn our ways and do as we do. They learn our ways and do *better* than we do. Maybe some of us ought to be assimilating with them.

Why "Let's Deport Them!"

Doesn't Work Now and Ain't Gonna Work Ever

One of the most entertaining fictions gamboling about in the current debate about illegal, mostly Mexican, immigration is that we should deport these 12 million souls back to their country of origin and make them apply for readmission as "guest workers."

This is particularly popular among many members of Congress, who don't have to intersect with reality on a daily basis and consequentially enjoy a form of Congressional Immunity from the real world. It also has its adherents in the West Wing of the White House, another protected refuge from the real world. But like the Tooth Fairy, a fiction that is widespread and enduring doesn't make it any less fictional.

As we mentioned at the start, deporting—or moving, feeding, housing,—12 million of any people is a non-trivial task. Not to mention sanitation and medicine and security. Look at the Katrina fiasco of 2005 and recall that, for the most part, these folks were citizens with regular names and addresses (albeit some under water), and fluent and literate in American English; and were about one-twentieth of the number of illegal immigrants.

But these 12 million mostly Mexican folks we would deport are foreigners and our government is in control, right? Well, could be, but if our government is in control, then how in the hell did these 12 million illegal immigrants get here in the first place? Our government, for the most part, is taking the position taken by each of two toddlers when their mother walks into a room with a broken vase: "he did it!"

So let's suspend disbelief, which is required for reading fantasy novels and government pronouncements. Let's assume that the Wicked Witch of The Southwest waves her wand and all the illegals go back home. What happens then?

A few things, none of them pleasant:

- Service and construction industries take it in the shorts. That raises the cost of both services and construction for those companies able to find natives willing and capable. Suggestions that native Americans will now fill those jobs are revealed as the pipe dreams they always were—if native Americans had been available and willing and at the same price, the illegal immigrants wouldn't have filled those jobs in the first place.

- Mexico, which has survived its grotesquely unequal distribution of wealth and power by not only permitting, but tacitly encouraging illegal immigration to the U.S., gets a social problem it is absolutely unable to handle without violence. A Mexico that makes about as much from "remittances" as it does from oil exports would have both financial and social bomb fuses ignited with consequences unknowable except that they certainly wouldn't be good.

- The deported illegals, although understandably ticked off that their struggle for a better life got dumped through the down chute, would wait a couple of months and come back, because they understand that they are filling a need in a willing marketplace and that if they are diligent, discrete—and, admittedly, lucky—their children and their children's children will have lives of opportunity and plenty that could only be imagined in the *pueblo*.

Why those deported, whether by the Wicked Witch of the Southwest or a wicked Congress of the United States would come back—and left Mexico in the first place—is worth an examination.

A good way to start is to look at the U.S. northern border and our neighbor, Canada, and compare it to Mexico on the U.S. southern border. We see many Mexicans coming to the U.S. illegally. We don't see that many Canadians. Why is that?

Time to do a comparison table. All these numbers are from the CIA World Factbook and may differ slightly from other estimates here. As we've said, estimates are just that, and different estimators come up with different numbers.

And in advance, an apology for using percentages, which can be confusing in comparisons. But percentages trump actual numbers, which can be bigger liars than government economists when they are used to compare groups of greatly different sizes. To say that "50 percent of the population lives in abject poverty" is equally true if you are talking about a village of 100 souls and a nation of 100 million—but comparable in ways only a calculator would recognize.

That concludes today's Figures Lie and Liars Figure lecture, so back to the table:

Canada	Mexico
Area: 9,984,670 sq km—a bit larger than the U.S.	Area: 1,972,550 sq km—almost three times the size of Texas, or France.
Land Use: arable (you can farm it) land 4.57 percent	Land Use: Arable land 12.66 percent.
Population: 33,098,932 (July '06 estimate)	Population: 107,449,525 (July '06 estimate)
Birth Rate: 10.78 births/1,000 population	Birth Rate: 20.69 births/ 1,000 population
Net Immigration Rate: 5.85 migrants/ 1,000 population	Net Immigration Rate: -4.32 migrants/1,000 population (More leave than come)
GDP Purchasing Power Parity:	GDP Purchasing Power Parity:

$1.114 trillion	$1.068 trillion
GDP Real Growth Rate: 2.9 percent (2005 estimate)	GDP Real Growth Rate: 3 percent (2005 estimate)

So between Canada and Mexico, Canada has a lot more land but most folks know you can't grow much on permafrost or ice. Mexico has more than three times more citizens. But the way Mother Nature arranged it, Mexico must try to feed those citizens on a bit more than half the arable land of Canada (about 456,000 sq km for Canada and 250,000 for Mexico). And maybe it's just too cold in Canada, but the birth rate in Mexico is almost twice that of Canada.

Purchasing power parity GDP between the two U.S. neighbors is close to even. And while Canada has two official languages, French and English, and the cultural baggage that goes with both, Mexico has no federal-level official language, but Spanish is the de facto national tongue and there are linguistic and cultural roots both from Europe and pre-colonial times. In fact, some Mexicans from the poorer and more heavily indigenous southern parts of Mexico don't speak fluent Spanish any more than they speak fluent English or Farsi.

So how come the number of Canadians moving south, most legally, is a lot smaller than the number of Mexicans moving north, most illegally? Take a look at the next table.

Canada	Mexico
Household Income or consumption by percentage share: lowest 10 percent—2.8 percent; highest 10 percent—23.8 percent (1994)	Household Income or consumption by percentage share: lowest 10 percent—1.6 percent; highest 10 percent—35.6 percent (2002)
Population Below Poverty Line: 15.9 percent, but Canada doesn't have an official poverty line and their Low-Income Cut-	Population Below Poverty Line: 40 percent (2003 estimate)

Off (LICO) gives a figure higher than comparable economies.	
Exports: U.S. 85.1 percent	Exports: U.S. 87.6 percent
Imports: U.S. 58.9 percent	Imports: U.S. 55.1 percent

Gee, these two neighbors sell us roughly the same amount of stuff, and they buy roughly the same amount of stuff. So why aren't Canadians sneaking across the border?

Part of the answer is in the tables.

First, look at the "population below poverty line" estimates and then apply them to that country's population. For Canada, that works out to about 5.26 million. For Mexico, it's about 43 million. Or, putting it another way, there are more poor folks in Mexico than there are folks in Canada period.

Then, look at the income distribution estimates at the low end, where it matters. In Canada, a "poor" person is getting 57 percent more of the national pie than a counterpart in Mexico.

Differences in social systems, government programs and government efficiency make this whole topic one for some struggling graduate student seeking to get a degree by doing the professor's publishing work. But the thing to take from here is that the poor in Mexico are both poorer than their counterparts in Canada and much more numerous.

Some will speak of that as a greater incentive, some will see it as a greater desperation, but however characterized, the United States has got, by most estimates, 12 million illegal immigrants, 85 percent of them from Mexico.

In Mexico, the old saw that "the rich get richer while the poor get poorer" is literally true. And it's unlikely to change. Economic divisions are largely along class lines, which in Mexico, are largely along racial lines. Those of (mostly) Spanish/European origin live lives apart, insulated from their countrymen by gates, guards, culture and wealth.

Unless otherwise identified, they are virtually indistinguishable from any other group of European stock. But as we've said, that description doesn't fit nine out of ten of their countrymen. There are conditions that the rest of their countrymen face which suggest why they leave, and why, except for visits or retirement, they aren't willing to come back.

Condition One—Crime: Crime in Mexico is not out of control because there is ample evidence to suggest it was never in control in the first place. The ruling oligarchy insulates itself from the crime faced by ordinary citizens—and ordinary tourists—by living the G3-protected lives common to most ruling classes: Gates, Guards, Guns.

For those not in the gated villas or armored limousines, it's a different story.

The murder rate—at least the reported one—for Mexico in 2000, according to a United Nations survey, was 14.11 per 100,000 population. The corresponding U.S. rate in the same year, the FBI says, was 5.5. Granted that the first impulse of a murderer surveying his or her crime is not to run to a statistician, that is a chilling figure. To put it in pop-speak, our neighbor with one-third our land area and a bit more than a third of our population has three times the United States murder rate.

Games may be played with numbers, but it's worth reading what Mexico's two North American Free Trade Association (NAFTA) partners were advising their citizens about visiting Mexico. Here's what Ottawa's Department of Foreign affairs and International Trade was telling Canadians about visiting Mexico in June of 2006:[iv]

"Caution and prudence should be exercised at all times while traveling throughout the country. Random shootings involving Canadians have occurred in areas notorious for drug trafficking. Other crimes occur, including armed robbery, purse snatching, and pickpocketing. You should dress down and avoid wearing expensive jewelry and designer clothing. Carry only the cash or credit cards that will be needed on each outing.

"Canadians should exercise extreme caution when traveling in areas where organized crime and urban violence have affected the region's security, such as in the northern region of Mexico and the state of Guerrero. While Canadians have not been specific targets of crime, they are urged to be aware of safety concerns when visiting the border area. . .

"Travelers should be careful when accepting food or drinks from strangers, as there have been cases of drugging followed by robbery and assault, including sexual assault. Avoid walking after dark, especially if traveling alone. Unpatrolled beaches and unpopulated areas should be avoided, especially after dark. Check with local authorities to determine which beaches are safe, but always remain alert.

"Long term kidnappings occur, although foreigners are not specifically targeted. So called "express kidnappings" are frequent in urban areas. There have been many incidents, particularly in Mexico City, of passengers being assaulted and/or robbed and/or car jacked by thieves working in co-operation with, or posing as taxi drivers. A common practice is to force victims to withdraw money from various ATMs with their bank or credit cards in exchange for their release. You should be cautious and discrete about openly discussing your financial or business affairs.

"Canadians should be cautious in general when withdrawing funds from ATMs or when exchanging money at a "casa de cambio". It is safer to withdraw only small sums for anticipated expenses and if possible to limit your withdrawals to daylight hours inside shops or malls, rather than at ATMs on the street. Be attentive when leaving an exchange bureau, as there are incidents of people being followed and attacked. If you are arriving at the airport in Mexico City and need to obtain pesos, use the exchange counters or ATMs in the arrival area, where public access is restricted.

70

"Women should exercise caution in dealing with strangers or recent acquaintances, and be especially careful about accepting rides or invitations to go for a drink. There have been cases of drugging followed by robbery and assault, including sexual assault. Incidents of assault, rape and sexual aggression against foreigners have been reported at beach resorts in Mexico. Many of these have occurred at night or in the early morning hours. Attacks have also occurred on deserted beaches and in hotel rooms. Acquaintance rape is a serious problem. In some cases, hotel workers, taxi drivers, and others have been implicated . . .

"Although public transportation is relatively safe, take precautions at public transportation facilities, including airports, bus stations, and the Mexico City metro, and avoid travelling during rush hour if you can.

"Be wary of persons presenting themselves as police officers. There have been instances of tourists becoming victims of theft, extortion or sexual assault by persons who may or may not be police officers. Some criminals pose as plainclothes police officers and ask to see foreign currency and passports. In Cancun, there have been cases involving legitimate police officers extorting money from tourists and arresting tourists for minor offenses. . ."

Hardly a sales pitch, eh?

The United States Department of State sings a similar song:

"CRIME: Crime in Mexico continues at high levels, and it is often violent, especially in Mexico City, Tijuana, Ciudad Juarez, Nuevo Laredo, and the state of Sinaloa. Other metropolitan areas have lower, but still serious, levels of crime. Low apprehension and conviction rates of criminals contribute to the high crime rate. Travelers should always leave valuables and irreplaceable items in a safe place, or not bring them. All visitors are encouraged to make use of hotel safes when available, avoid wearing obviously expensive jewelry or designer clothing, and carry only the cash or credit cards that will be needed on each outing. There are a significant number of pick-pocketing incidents, purse snatchings and hotel-room thefts. Public transportation is a particularly popular place for pickpockets. .

"Visitors should be aware of their surroundings at all times, even when in areas generally considered safe. Women traveling alone are especially vulnerable and should exercise caution, particularly at night. Victims, who are almost always unaccompanied, have been raped, robbed of personal property, or abducted and then held while their credit cards were used at various businesses and Automatic Teller Machines (ATMs). Armed street crime is a serious problem in all of the major cities. Some bars and nightclubs, especially in resort cities such as Cancun, Cabo San Lucas, Mazatlan, and Acapulco, can be havens for drug dealers and petty criminals. Some establishments may contaminate or drug drinks to gain control over the patron.

"U.S. citizens should be very cautious in general when using ATMs in Mexico. If an ATM must be used, it should be accessed only during the business day at large protected facilities (preferably inside commercial establishments, rather than at glass-enclosed, highly visible ATMs on streets). U.S. and Mexican citizens are sometimes accosted on the street and forced to withdraw money from their accounts using their ATM cards.

"Kidnapping, including the kidnapping of non-Mexicans, continues at alarming rates. So-called "express" kidnappings, an attempt to get quick cash in exchange for the release of an individual, have occurred in almost all the large cities in Mexico and appear to target not only the wealthy, but also middle class persons. . .

"Criminal assaults occur on highways throughout Mexico; travelers should exercise extreme caution at all times, avoid traveling at night. . ."

So if the governments of both Canada and the U.S. are telling their citizens that Mexico isn't the safest place to visit, imagine what the majority of Mexicans are telling each other.

They can tell each other whatever they like as long as they don't anger or interfere with the drug cartels, who maintain a lucrative trade through business practices that make the Mafia seem like a day-school playground bunch.

In a March 2006 report, the U.S. Department of State said 70 to 90 percent of cocaine aimed at the United States passes through Mexico or its periphery. Mexico is also a big supplier of marijuana and methamphetamine, with meth being the growth product as U.S. efforts put the squeeze on domestic sources.

This means big money. An August 2005 article in the Christian Science Monitor said "Mexican drug lords are calling the shots in what the UN estimates is a $142 billion a year business. The competition for that pie among the major drug cartels is mostly expressed in violence. That same article reported that the US Consulate in Nuevo Laredo was closed for a week because of "a downtown shootout between Mexican traffickers involving high-powered rifles, rocket-propelled grenades and bazookas." The United States itself is not immune to drug wars, as it wasn't immune during prohibition to whiskey wars. But as far as I am able to determine, no foreign consulate in the U.S. has been closed because of a forecast of "continued intermittent Rocket-Propelled-Grenades, with occasional high-powered rifle fire punctuated by the odd bazooka round."

Border newspapers and blogs consistently report that the violence crosses the border sometimes in the form of former commandoes, some said to be US Army trained, called Los Zetas. Other reports identify the cross-border enforcers as corrupt elements of the Mexican Army.

WordNetDaily.com reported in June 2005 that "A U.S. Justice Department memo says the U.S.-trained units have recently moved operations into Houston,

San Antonio and the states of California, Oklahoma, Tennessee, Georgia and Florida. They have been operating in Dallas for at least two years, according to the feds." If that's the case, perhaps we should make them part of the DEA, the Drug Enforcement Administration. Sure, they're enforcing a different aspect of the drug trade, but they were obviously organized enough to get here while U.S. federal agents weren't organized enough to keep them out. Score: Creeps 1, Inepts 0.

Although under intense U.S. political pressure to reduce the drug trade, the government of Vicente Fox has only recently stepped up enforcement efforts, and those results are questionable. Part of that is because while political pressure makes the stuff of nice newspaper editorials, only economic or military pressure can alter behavior between governments. The Soviet Union dissolved because it couldn't stay in the arm/economic poker game with NATO, not because the commissars had sudden democratic conversions.

In Mexico, government officials thunder against the drug trade. And yes, drug lords are in prison. But if you have lots of money, being in a Mexican prison needn't crimp your business or even your lifestyle. It's called corruption, and it's the second major condition that must be considered in thinking about Mexico today and tomorrow.

Condition Two—Corruption: The law in Mexico is essentially a product list and getting it either enforced or ignored is set at a price in the marketplace. This is not at all unusual in what we have come to call the Third World, but we try to avoid remembering it because, well, it's awkward being a neighbor with the Third World on the southern border and the First World on the north. There are, have been, and will be corrupt United States and Canadian officials, but their honest counterparts far and away outnumber the stinkers. In Mexico, corruption takes a different face.

Corruption is so much part of the fabric of daily existence in Mexico that it can't be ignored. And, quite probably, it can't be eliminated. As Lennox Samuels reported in the December 28, 2005 Dallas Morning News article about corruption in Mexico:

"... corruption is so deeply embedded in the society that there's no prospect of eliminating or even curbing it anytime soon.

" 'Unfortunately, corruption seems to be part of our DNA,' said political analyst Jorge Chabat."

Part of DNA probably not, but a direct consequence of the economic disparity most certainly. If you are a policeman in Mexico City and stop someone for driving the wrong way on a one-way street, you can write that person a ticket. Or, you can supplement your meager income by accepting a nice "fine" on the spot. And if you are the unfortunate driver, your choice is to pay a large sum now, or pay larger and larger sums as you wend your way through what it laughably called the justice system. Humans being humans, you can guess which impulses prevail on either side.

When corruption is epidemic in any society, it is not limited in the least to the daily small transactions of ordinary citizens uniting Those Who Take and Those Who Give.

On June 12, 2006, The Wall Street Journal ran an article on how then 2006 Mexican presidential candidate Felipe Calderón's brother-in-law seems to have won $223 million in government contracts while Calderón served briefly as energy minister. Lucky guy, maybe, at the least, energetic.

But the most telling thing was that the Journal also ran a box so readers would understand that several presidents of Mexico, from Vicente Fox back to Manuel Ávila Camacho in 1940 seem to have had relatives who were embarrassing, and, for some, judging by the dollar amounts alleged, either very industrious or very, very lucky. Indeed, in the last presidential election, both the half-whisker victorious camp of Calderón, and the hundreds of thousands of disappointed backers of Andrés

Manuel López Obrador threw charges of corruption.

In that they were both very probably right is a perverse assurance that the election count was real. With an equal opportunity to load the dice, and lifelong skills at doing so, it's not hard to see that corruption was evenly spread and so had no appreciable say in the final court-certified election total.

Global Integrity, a Washington, DC-based group that advocates and measures government integrity, has a few tidbits about Mexico. One of the most interesting they cite is an April 2002 United Nations reports they say estimates that "50 percent to 70 percent of Mexican judges are corrupt." They also cite a different report in the same month that says corruption sucks seven percent of Mexico's GDP. (Other estimates run higher.)

This is not to say that Mexico has a monopoly on government corruption. As the late Chicago newspaper columnist Mike Royko was fond of saying, Chicago's official motto was "Urbs in Horto"

(City In A Garden), but the real one was "Ubi Est Mea"—Where's Mine?

The obvious difference is in the degree of penetration throughout society in both levels and functions. Yes, the relatives and friends of senior elected or appointed officials in Mexico seem to be astoundingly lucky, but so do the building inspectors, policemen, sanitation engineers—anyone who has a Yes/No power is charging if you want to influence which choice is made.

According to a PBS report, a Mexican-conducted survey in 2000 found that "In Mexico City, for every 100 public services, 22.6 percent (of the 38 administrative procedures tracked) in the survey required bribes."

A 2004 paper, *"About the decisions to commit corruption in Mexico: the role of perceptions, individual and social effects"* has some interesting observation. The first of which is the author, Manuel Alejandro Guerrero Eduardo Rodríguez-Oreggia of Universidad Iberoamericana in Mexico City is pretty much immune from the charge that his observations are just more Mexican-bashing from racist Yanquis.

He first cites the "2004 International Transparency Corruptions Perceptions Index," which is how an academic says "How Crooked Are Those Guys ?" and reports that Mexico ranks 64 out of 146 countries. Mexico's score was 3.6 on a scale of 1 to 10, higher scores meaning least corrupt.

Like many things academic, this can be misleading, but the ordinary human assessment of corruption in Mexico comes from quotes taken in focus groups for the study:

- "In Mexico if you are not corrupt; you are an idiot... You know, as the saying goes, *if you do not cheat, you do not progress*. A typical way of thought here... A way of living for many groups of people, for many of us".
- "(*Mordida*) is a payment, is a kind of effective way of getting back a favor, or of making the authority turn its head elsewhere while you

83

do something you should not do" (*Mordida* translates as "bite.")

- "Corruption exists across the board in the government—from top to bottom; not only the police; and we know how to deal with it...by paying.
- "You cannot justify corruption, but in a country where even politicians constantly break the rules, well, you know..."

The translation to English comes from an English version of the study supplied by its author and available on the net. Although you'll sometimes be swimming upstream in academic jargon, it's well worth the effort. Find it in .pdf format at:
www.uia.mx/campus/publicaciones/IIDSES/idses9.pdf

The final tidbit on corruption comes from George W. Grayson, who teaches government at the College of William and Mary. In a March 2006 article in the Christian Science Monitor, he observes that bribes in 2004 totaled $11.2 billion, about 12 percent of the Mexican GDP. For some perspective, note that taxes from government at all levels run around the 25 percent level of the US GDP.

Grayson also says in the same article that education got just 5.3 percent of the Mexican GDP and healthcare just 6.1 percent. And, most damningly, he adds: "When oil revenues are excluded, Mexico raises the equivalent of only nine percent of its gross domestic product in taxes—a figure roughly equivalent to that of Haiti and far below the level of major Latin American nations."

Condition Three—Feudalism Lives: When you begin reading the available commentary and exposition on modern Mexico, it won't take you long to realize that you often encounter a word seldom used in United States discourse: *peasants*.

Imagine someone running for Congress in the United States promising to "uphold the interests of the peasants." So what the heck is a peasant, if we're not talking Middle Ages?

Merriam-Webster defines "peasant" this way:

"1: a member of a European class of persons tilling the soil as small landowners or as laborers, also: a member of a similar class elsewhere

2: a usually uneducated person of low social status."

Unsaid by Merriam-Webster, but implicit in the life of Mexico is the corollary that peasants are a class, part of a system of boxes in which society consigns inhabitants at birth—and spends considerable energy to keep them from crawling out of the boxes, ever, and most especially from one box to the next one above.

There is nothing in the 1917 Mexican constitution that prohibits upward mobility, pretty much like the United States constitution of more than a century earlier. What inhibits peasants crawling out of their box and into the middle class amounts to lack of jobs paying a living wage, almost-overt class and racial discrimination by the entrenched elite and abysmal education and health care for between 40 and 50 percent of Mexico's citizens.

When Vicente Fox was elected president in 2000, it was universally hailed as the end of a period of one-party rule, which was simply silly. Yes, the party of the President of Mexico had changed from the seven-decade rule of the Institutional Revolutionary Party (PRI) to the National Action Party (PAN) but the rule of Mexico's elite remained absolutely unchanged. The 90 percent of Mexicans who are of either mixed Amerindian or pure Amerindian blood now had a chief of Irish/Spanish ancestry, one who had a university education and started as a route supervisor for the Coca-Cola company, rising to head Coke's operations first in Mexico and then all of Latin America. Not exactly up-from-adversity or rags-to-riches.

Felipe Calderón is a man of similar background. He got a bachelor's degree in law and a master's in economics from Mexican institutions of higher learning and topped that with a master's degree in public administration from Harvard University's Kennedy School of Government. Not exactly a typical story for Mexico's millions.

Of course, his main opponent, López Obrador was different. From López Obrador's website biography we find: *"López Obrador was born on November 13, 1953, in the southern Mexican State of Tabasco, an oil rich location with abundant natural resources. He was raised in a middle class family. A former altar boy, he grew up inspired by the Lone Ranger and his hard-working parents. An avid baseball fan, he usually played the center field position and once considered becoming a professional player. . .*

"A prolific book writer, López Obrador received a Bachelor's degree in political science from the National University of Mexico (UNAM)."

Those of appropriate age will recall that the Longer Ranger was assisted by his faithful Indian sidekick Tonto, but will resist applying the memory to the demographics of Lone Ranger-inspired López Obrador's support in the 2006 election.

López Obrador, Fox and Calderón have life stories that are so foreign to almost half of the Mexican population who are poor by Mexican standards, they might as well be about the political rise of little green men from the canals of Mars, whose relatives all somehow got exclusive barge shipping rights.

Because American myth—not to mention American fact—is filled with rags-to-riches tales of poor folk who worked and studied hard, made the most of their luck and rose to great prominence, it is hard for U.S. persons to understand that Mexico—indeed, most of the world—does not work that way. Those who rule, whether by force of arms or force of class and discrimination have no interest in making the rags-to-riches model active. Democracy, from the Greek, literally means "rule by the people," and it should not be surprising that those who rule the people by right of birth and class have little real interest in it happening. This results in an interesting social model for the Mexican lower classes: The good sons and daughters in the lower classes do not become doctors or lawyers in Mexico, they slip into the United States and send money home. They key word there is "home."

"Home" is Mexico for many immigrants, illegal and otherwise, no matter how long they have toiled and lived in New Jersey, Nebraska, California, Arizona or elsewhere. It's where they would like to retire if they could earn the money to do so—and indeed, earning the money was what brought them here in the first place.

This fits so neatly into the model that is generally accepted as the end of feudalism in Europe that it is almost spooky. When European peasants became unbound to a feudal lord, and then to an inherited spot on the land, the fuses of change were lit over Europe. But it was change of a degree.

Those who could be comfortable in the then-norms of whatever society bore them, may have sought their fortunes overseas in the various colonies, but it was always with the intention of returning. A minority emigrated permanently. The fact that in the American Revolution, a significant number of loyalists refused to give up the British Crown they had hoped to see again, or see firmly planted in the so-called New World, attests to that.

So it is with many Mexican immigrants in the United States. They are not here longing for political freedom. They can vote freely, since 2000, for the candidate of their choice with some confidence that the vote is transparent and correct. That was the verdict of international observers on the 2006 presidential election, although one not shared by López Obrador and his supporters. Yet "We wuz robbed!" is as much a tradition of the democratic process as any other, provided that the actions—not the rhetoric—boil down to "Wait until next time!"

But many Mexican voters also think that whatever candidate they elect, unless completely radical, is acceptable if instead of being made better, their lives are simply not made worse. So they come to the United States to make money. And the dream for many is to return to home—Mexico—as moneyed folk, a home they left as poor peasants.

The point, and it is a significant one, is that working in the U.S., legally or otherwise, is the prime path of upward mobility for Mexico's peasants stuck in a social system that was supposed to have died around 1800. They have few or no upward paths in their own land, rich in resources as it is. The path to advancement and a comfortable old age invariably leads northward.

The intelligent and young and enterprising take it. The rest, at the bottom half of Mexican society, stay home and count on those money-transfers from the U.S.

But the money-transfers from the U.S. are no less counted upon by the ruling elite, which is why the government of Mexico is so solicitous about United States moves to tighten up illegal immigration. First, of course, there's the money, earned in the U.S., some significant portion of which, is spent in Mexico.

But most importantly, immigration of any flavor to the United States is the safety valve that keeps Mexican society from exploding. In a land where 40 to 50 percent of the population is poor and indigenous or mixed, and the top 8 or 9 percent of the population, mostly of pure European heritage is rich, the formula for social dynamite is ubiquitous and very explosive—unless, of course, there's an outlet, an alternative to rising up in revolution.

Illegal immigration to the U.S. had been supplying that alternative, that safety valve, and the feudal lords of Mexico's elite have zero interest in changing the status quo.

If you doubt it, look to the severe measures the government of Mexico employs to prevent illegal immigrants from Central and South America from entering Mexico's southern border on the long, difficult journey to the United States.

Maybe it's because the Mexican government truly believes in the sanctity of international borders.

Or maybe it's because self-preservation suggests that if there's going to be any illegal border crossing to the U.S. from Mexico, it's going to be done by Mexicans, not those foreign folks. This speculation is buttressed by Mexico's issuing "How To" pamphlets for those considering the trip.

A Spanish version of "Illegal Border Crossing and Employment For Dummies" hasn't been published—yet. But unless Mexican social conditions change, it would be a hot seller.

Why Not Just Fix Mexico?

So if Mexicans are flocking to the U.S. by the millions because of economic need, wouldn't they stay home if they could earn the same in Mexico as they do here? Why don't Mexicans just stay home and fix things?

That view is classical American thinking. If there's a problem, let's fix it. *"The difficult we do immediately; the impossible takes a little longer."*

Racial segregation along black versus everyone-else lines was a monumental problem for the United States 100 years after the Civil War. It was thought to be so deeply ingrained in society that nothing would ever change it. But the last two secretaries of state of the United States of America have been African-

Americans, and the current one a woman at that, making her the second female to hold that high and revered office. And while the problem isn't "fixed" completely, the progress is such that a visitor from America of 1946, dropped by magic into the America of 2006 would be as uncomfortable as a dog dropped on a distant planet ruled by cats.

As a boy in Cleveland, Ohio, in the 50s, I developed a lifelong affection for Brazil nuts. In the stores, they were labeled "Nigger Toes." Since we all smoked, or tried to, sharing cigarettes was a passage of youth. Of course, you were admonished by your buddies not to "nigger-lip" the shared "fag," getting it all wet with your saliva. This sort of thing could go on for a considerable time for any American—white or black—in their late 50s or beyond, but today we would pretty much all acknowledge that these are memories from another time, almost another planet, and belong there in any case.

So if the United States can end segregation by law, come reasonably close to ending it by custom and continue moving towards an integrated, equal-opportunity society, why don't the Mexicans get busy?

Maybe because they are already busy being Mexicans, and we're too dumb to note the difference. The American attitude that folk in other countries are really just Americans who talk funny, sets us up to ignore fundamental cultural differences, that generate different outcomes than we expected.

This was vividly illustrated in June of 2005 when the government of Vicente Fox—he's a reformer, remember—issued a series of stamps honoring *Memin Pinguin,* a beloved comic book character from the 1940s whose magazines still sell more than 100,000 copies weekly. A look at some of the stamps speaks for itself[v]:

The stamps, worth about 60 cents US for first-class postage drew howls of outrage north of the border and absolute puzzlement south of it. For U.S. eyes, the thick lips, wide eyes and exaggerated features screamed Little Boy Sambo racism. Investigation of the comics themselves showed the obviously black character was kidded by white characters, about his speech, dress, and other attributes. In general, the stamp issue got the same reception that might greet a prime-time revival of the Amos N' Andy radio programs, done for TV by white actors in blackface.

And it was no particular help that in May of 2006, President Fox complained that Mexicans in the U.S. were taking jobs that "not even blacks" want.

The White House spokesman at the time, Scott McClellan, said the stamps were an internal matter for Mexico, but added: "Racial stereotypes are offensive no matter what their origin. The Mexican government needs to take this into account. Images like these have no place in today's world."

Well, maybe not in today's world in the United States, but they certainly did in Mexico, where they were not considered racist.

Or as CBS News reported at the time, ". . . Ruben Aguilar, a spokesman for President Vicente Fox, said the comic book has promoted understanding and family values for decades and deserved to be enshrined on a stamp.

" 'It seems strange to me that this celebration of Mexican culture and Mexico's post office's toast to Mexican cartoonists is misunderstood,' he said."

The buzz ran around the world and a New Zealand television station, TV One, reported *"Mexico, which has few blacks and considers racism much less of an issue, is baffled at the US reaction. It said the stamps were a harmless tribute to a popular Mexican cartoon.*

"Mexican Foreign Minister Luis Ernesto Derbez told reporters the US response was "totally incorrect."

"Memin Pinguin is a character with a long tradition in our culture," he said.

"He is loved by all Mexicans and it shows a complete lack of understanding of our culture that people are translating this to their culture with no respect for ours."

That Mexicans can and do refer to their fellow citizens by terms that can be translated as "Whitey," "Blackie," or "Brownie" with no offense given on taken is a mystery on this side of the Rio Grande right up there with Jimmy Hoffa's grave site. Similar speech in the U.S. would have a better-than-even chance of putting you up on hate-speech charges, and an almost sure shot at getting told where you could keep your opinions with eager volunteers to put them there.

If the differences in perception over a stamp honoring a popular cartoon character can echo around the world, it is important to understand the other differences on more important stuff.

One of those is world view, the expectations that all of us have about our role in the world and our future.

While almost all the world rightly abhors torture of humans or animals, torturing analogies is still fair game, so let's put a couple in the spotlight and torture them. At this writing, analogies have no legal standing in any court.

First, the world view of most Americans, whether by birth or affirmation, sees society as a stairway. We all start someplace on the stairway, but through education, hard work, help and luck, we can finish our lives on a much higher stair and pass the boost on to our children. Another common expression of this view is "the race," often "the rat race," and it is exactly this race for advancement and material gain that those "dropout hippies" of the 60s and 70s were dropping out of running.

There are other ways of looking at life. Suppose it's not a stairway or a race—suppose it's a sorting-box in a giant mailroom and you get put into your box at birth and stay there, unless, by rare mistake, The Great Sorter put you in the wrong box.

With that view, you don't seek happiness in a different box, you seek it in your own box. Oh, you may have to go out of the box for a time to earn money, but your goal is always to bring it back. That may be a summary of the view of many—maybe most—of the illegal immigrants, mostly Mexicans, whose tens of millions have Uncle Sam's knickers in a very tight twist.

The key factoid is the 20 billion dollars they send home every year. Sure, immigrant groups have always helped the folks back home. But if you were looking to make your life here, you probably wouldn't be sending half or more of what you are able to earn back to the homeland. which suggests that the millions of Mexicans who are working here don't wish to become Americans as much as they wish to become comfortable Mexicans in the box that Mexi-

can society has assigned them. They
don't want to leave their country as
much as they want to earn enough
money to live in their country.

If that is the case, they differ from
previous immigrants in significant ways,
one of which is that return is a possibility. The blacks who were hauled here in
chains that would ultimately bind both
captor and captive couldn't return. The
Europeans and Asians who fled starva-
tion and/or totalitarianism couldn't go
back.

Oh, they tried to recreate the homeland in Chinatown, Germantown, Little
Italy, Greektown, Little Poland, Little
Russia, Little Korea, what have you, but
even that was an implicit admission that
they weren't going back. You do not
build an imitation, however dear, if you
have access to the real thing.

The society for which they long is not
ours, and they might not long for it if it
were.

An interesting case in point s what
happened to Mexico's corn and bean
growers in the aftermath of NAFTA.

First, understand that corn and beans, in whatever form, furnish the basic nutrients for most of Mexico. In pre-revolutionary France, it would have been the bread for which Marie Antoinette is said to have offered a cake alternative—and in Mexico today, just as politically charged.

Now remember that 25 percent of Mexicans are still farmers. Of those farmers in August 2003, according to foodfirst.org, subsistence farmers accounted for 45 percent of all Mexican corn-growing. Subsistence means they are growing corn as it has been grown for thousands of years—poor soil, rain-dependent, few storage facilities and fewer marketing channels. Now enter NAFTA, with huge, mechanized American farms, heavily government-subsidized and production that would rival the hordes of Midas.

Well, of course, that drove down the price of corn, one of the two the basic Mexican staples. In the United States, where the family farm exists mostly as a thing of remembrance, the farm logic would have offered these alternatives:

1. Grow another, more profitable crop,
2. Grow less corn because the return isn't worth the investment, so the net to not grow might be the same as growing.
3. See if there's a factory hiring, or a more fortunate farmer hiring, and check to see if Uncle Silas's lung problem has gotten worse.

In Mexico, things are different. When NAFTA's 800-pound gorilla dropped the price of corn, subsistence farmers *increased* the acreage for that crop. That is because growing corn is not seen as a business proposition as much as it is seen as a lifestyle. The situation with beans was not much different, or as the United States Department of Agriculture (USDA) observed in 2003, "The future of dry bean production in Mexico is in question. Inconsistent weather patterns and economic stress threaten to make it unprofitable in many states."

In the United States, if corn is not profitable, even with massive government subsidies, you grow something else or bag it all and find other work. In Mexico, accepting the letter-box in which you were first slotted, you grow corn or beans because that's what you are—a corn grower or a bean-grower. And if the corn or beans you grow doesn't earn enough to keep you from poverty, you are a poor corn-grower or bean-grower.

That smacks of class-bound conservatism and will rile the liberal hound-pack, but it addresses a question seldom asked in American political debate: *Do these masses _want_ to change?* The American national assumption is that they do; the reality may be different. And the also-unspoken assumptions that they could change no matter the circumstance, and that they live in a society that permits it, demand intelligent questioning.

In July 2005, the Wall Street Journal in an article by David Luhnow and John Lyons, published two paragraphs, part of which sums it up nicely:

". . .The son of a blue-collar worker in Mexico has only a 10 percent chance of making the jump to a white-collar job, compared with a 30 percent chance in the U.S. . . .

"Because of an abundance of natural resources and a large indigenous population, Latin American nations grew up relying on raw materials, cheap manual labor to exploit them and low government taxation. The system concentrated land ownership and wealth in a few hands, deprived governments of money to spend on education and offered little incentive for the elite to invest in human capital or technology. Latin America has also historically relied on monopolies and franchises, leaving few opportunities for entrepreneurs to advance through hard work and innovation: The American dream never became the Latin American dream."

That ought to be engraved on the forehead of every member of Congress who steps up to make pronouncements on the immigration issue. Of course, if they only mingled with other members of Congress, who would ever read it?

It also ought to be a theme of public discourse. If we accept that illegal Mexican immigrants aren't trying to become part of our society, just trying to make some money to help them and their families survive in their own society, the color and temperature of the debate changes. As a nation, as we said at the start, we have always been oopsie about immigration. But making money is universally understood and approved.

So our buddy Al. the prototypical Mexican immigrant, comes here and paints the houses, mows the lawns, washes the dishes and cleans the gutters, installs the insulation and fixes the roofs, and that gets him an income below U.S. poverty standards. "Below poverty standards" seriously upsets us, if "us" are the media who are generally from another planet, but condescend to report on this one. So the question becomes this: If our buddy Al just wants to earn enough money to go from being the poorest guy in Summit, NJ, to a very comfortable guy in his home pueblo, why do we have a problem with that?

Hasta La Vista
¡Reconquista!
¿Hola Anexión?
¡Madre de Dios!

Of the many whacko notions that abound in politics both north and south of the U.S./Mexican border, two enjoy a limited currency among those who write more than they read. First is the notion of *La Reconquista*, certainly a strong finalist for Dumbest of The Dumb Society's annual *Dum-De-Dum-Dum(D-quad) Cup*. Second is the flip side notion, that the U.S. annex Mexico, another strong D-quad contender.

Neither *La Reconquista* nor it's equally challenged sibling, *Annexation*, have any base in reality, but reality has never been a prerequisite for political opinions. One at a time, which probably challenges the math skills of their respective advocates:

Reconquista -- Simply put, this is the argument that since the lands like California, Arizona, New Mexico and other states or parts of states were originally part of Mexico, Mexico should "reconquer" those lands. As the Washington Times reported in an April 2006 article about the immigration reform protests, "One popular banner read 'If you think I'm illegal because I'm a Mexican, learn the true history because I'm in my homeland.'"

The provenance of La Reconquista is itself interesting. It's a reference to the medieval Christians finally getting it together to retake Spain and Portugal from the Moslem caliphate, which had invaded in 711 and stayed from then until the last Moorish enclave was captured in 1492.

That there may be just a few differences between the Moslem caliphate in the late Middle Ages and the United States of America in the 21st Century

110

seems to escape completely those who preach reconquista.

Not even the almost completely unstable firebrands speak of doing so by force. That's because Mexico has armed forces in about the same way a 17-year-old has independence, at the sufferance of the grownups.

The usual note is that Mexicans will simply ignore the border and move in until they become the majority. To sing in this chorus, you have to ignore more than the border, beginning with relevant math.

The US population reached the 300 million mark sometime in the summer of 2006 Even if every one of the estimated 107 million Mexicans moved across the border tomorrow morning and were immediately granted full citizenship rights, and voted as a solid block, they'd still amount to just a shade over 26 percent of the country, probably pretty much the same of the electorate.

Well, maybe they could outbreed us.

Over time—a long time—that's possible, but it assumes a couple of things about the fertility rate that may not pan out.

In a 2005 report, the Center for Immigration Studies reported that the number of children a Mexican woman could be expected to have during her reproductive years was 2.4 if she stayed in Mexico. If she became an immigrant to the United States, the number jumped to 3.51. If Americans visiting Mexico are advised to avoid drinking the water to avoid gastric distress, Mexicans immigrating to the United States ought to be advised of possible pregnancy.

In fairness, Mexicans aren't the only folk who seem to create more babies here than they do at home. The same study reports the total fertility in the United Kingdom (*"No sex please, we're British"*) to be 1.66 at home, but 2.84 if they move to the United States. *"Give me your tired, your poor, your horny. . ."* isn't part of the poem on the Statue of liberty, but the statistics are testimony that a free society, a society of more-or-less-level opportunity seem to flip the "let's make a baby" switch.

The only way this away-game blossoming of fertility could significantly aid La Reconquista is if Mexican immigrant fertility rates stayed at high levels across several generations. But the CIS says the fertility rate for illegals was about half again as high as for natives, and drops from 3.51 to 2.61 if you look at legal immigrants only.

The alarmists, both in the Reconquista battalions and in the Build Walls! ranks of U.S. natives seem to find it convenient to ignore change over time. The children of those who eluded the border patrol to illegally mow your lawn, if they are born here, wind up being educated in public schools, from kindergarten to universities. They will make enormous contributions to society, except in the family department, where they will join other educated folks— whether immigrants or native—in having a fertility rate of around 2. And oh yeah, the lawn that their parents mowed for others and the house around it? Their kids will probably buy it.

We've said that the "melting pot" is really a stew pot, and that the ingredients from everywhere complement each other's flavors while retaining their own identity. The informed bet is that would pretty much make Reconquista-by-pregnancy a non-starter.

For the record, here's a quick look at the military option, but that's not even up for consideration unless you've spent the afternoon enjoying some of the billions of dollars of drugs that run through Mexico.

The armed forces of Mexico number in total around 300,000, divided into two main groups, the Army, with a subordinate Air Force, and the Navy. Their primary mission is domestic, and the last time they flexed any sort of armed international muscle was in 1942, when an expeditionary force was sent to the Philippines after two Mexican ships were sunk and the Mexican Congress declared war on Nazi Germany and Imperial Japan.

It is not recorded whether Germany or Japan noticed.

The Mexican armed forces did provide disaster relief to Hurricane Katrina victims, marking the first time uniformed members of that corps have been on American soil since the Mexican-American war, but in this case with much better result. True, his legislature nipped at President Vicente Fox for sending Mexican troops to foreign soil without the required legislative permission, but he was able to ignore that on humanitarian grounds (not to mention the rich political benefit of the Third World sending help to the First).

In the domestic arena, Mexico's armed forces have mostly been used for internal security and disaster relief. They are dispersed across the country in 12 military regions and within those regions, 44 military zones that mostly correspond to the 31 Mexican states. Like the United States, the laws of Mexico frown on using armed forces for domestic law enforcement. And as in the United States, there are ways to live up to the letter of those laws while dancing on their spirit. A Mexican example:

In July of 2006, former Mexican President Luis Echeverría was placed under house arrest. The charge was genocide in reference to a 1968 massacre of students by the Army in Mexico City's Tlatelolco Plaza. Ailing and 84 when arrested, Echeverría was interior secretary in 1968. The estimates of those deaths just before the Mexican hosting of the Olympics range from 25 to 300, depending upon whether the estimators are from the government or human rights groups, but it is a current and vivid example of the real purpose of the Mexican armed forces—domestic control.

While Mexico has elite units, the majority of the forces are not as focused on military action as other duties. In fact, says Wikipedia, the required year-long military service for Mexican males is mostly civil and "takes only a few hours on weekends." And here's the clincher:

"Most Mexicans, for example, that have been recruited into the military,

116

have never touched a gun by the time their civil service is completed."

That is not, to put it mildly, the U.S. model.

If Wikipedia, the free web encyclopedia is to be believed, the armed forces of Mexico have a total of one-hundred-sixty 105-mm Howitzers. At any given time, the United States has about 4,000 tanks with either 105-mm or 120-mm cannons, never mind the endless string of self-propelled and towed Howitzers. Not to mention rockets and missiles, and bombs and . . .well, you get the picture. Mexico invading the U.S. militarily is not a realistic prospect, or if so, not a very long-lived prospect.

It is also not a realistic political prospect. The ruling oligarchies of Mexico have used the United States as an escape valve for years and have no intention of giving it up. In the 2006 presidential election, all five of the declared candidates had almost identical positions on U.S. immigration, legal or otherwise: they were for it. And they were also for stronger measures to safeguard the rights of Mexicans in the United States, never mind how they arrived. The 2006 victor, Felipe Calderon, tracks nicely with this line—as must any Mexican politician who can see the real world and has small intention of trying to change it.

This is not because of a humanitarian streak in the ruling classes. It is their accurate assessment that without an alternative, the many poor would become ungovernable by the rich few.

There may also be a realization that in the unlikely event of Reconquista, Mexico's political/government infrastructure would simply not be up to the task. If California were a nation, its Gross Domestic Product (GDP) would come in at around $1.5 trillion, easily putting it in the top ten of the world's giant economies, a club Mexico has yet to join. And given their record, a club that requires skills they do not yet possess.

And we should never forget that $20 billion a year—and growing monthly—that Mexicans in the United States are sending home. If we make the point again and again, it is not too often. The majority of Mexicans who come here aren't looking to settle here and retire here and be buried here. They just want to make some money to have a more comfortable life at home, and a death and burial in a society where even stiffs get a drink once a year on Día de los Muertos (Day of the Dead), a festival celebrating the reunion of dead relatives with their families, every November 1st and 2nd.

One dummy down, one to go.

Annex Mexico—This strong competitor to Reconquista for the D-quad cup say the modern United States should annex the rest of Mexico. The United States annexed half the country before, proponents argue—why not finish the job?

This notion thrives in the U.S. blogosphere in a roughly direct ratio to the political heat illegal immigration generates. You can even find "Annex Mexico" T-shirts for sale, the most observant slogan saying "It's a fixer upper—Annex Mexico."

Well, yes, we annexed a tad more than half of Mexico, and we later would buy Alaska, annex Hawaii, win Puerto Rico by force of arms, and pick up various other territories. But that was then, and this is now. And "now," for the benefit of the annexation crowd, no longer includes the 19th or the 20th centuries.

Sorry for the rude announcement folks, but we'll keep mum on Santa Clause, the Easter Bunny and the Tooth Fairy in return, okay?

Militarily, we could certainly annex the rest of Mexico. If we can project regime-changing force halfway around the world in Iraq and Afghanistan, we can do it in Mexico. Militarily, the armed forces of Mexico might be able to annoy a hundred thousand American troops, but certainly couldn't stop them from seizing key cities and government facilities.

And it's not like the United States hasn't a record of lusting after its neighbors. Canada was eyed with more than friendly interest for at least a century after 1776, and we've already examined our past with Mexico. But the reason a Mexican border guard with a machine pistol isn't already trying to face down an M1A1 Abrams Main Battle Tank is far more powerful than mere armed force. It's politics.

Any move to annex Mexico by force would have enormous political implications. Yes, that is like saying 'an H-bomb produces a really big explosion," but much of the political nonsense we see today may come as much from failing to state the obvious—and deal with it accordingly—as from any other source.

For Mexican politicians always seeking to wrap a deeply divided society in the duct tape of nationhood, it would be a great gift, a complete distraction from the mess they've made of a lovely country and people. And with a country that's about three times the size of Texas, and where American troops of occupation would be mostly as unable to blend as they are in Iraq, former criminals and drug lords would be transformed into noble resistance guerillas.

Mexico's geography lends itself to guerillas, whether noble or not. With both the east and west ranges of the Sierra Madres mountains dominating both coasts, and lots of sparsely populated desert, and some jungle, plus relatively few roads on which a modern army could move, the terrain is a significant advantage for those who want to strike from nowhere, return there and blend with the population. Besides, if the Mexicans themselves are unable to force either a political or military solution on the rebellious Zapatistas, there is little hope that United States Armed forces could do much better in the long run.

In world politics, the Death To America! Crowd would have itself a regular chant-fest, thronging square after square with howls of outrage, at least as long as there were cameras present. Our European and Asian close allies would studiously pretend to look the other way, as though we had passed gas at a

122

lawn party, and the countries of South America, among which we have few solid allies, would be torn between raising a diplomatic/public relations howl and half hoping they might be next. Ecuador and El Salvador might join the chorus of protest, for example, but the fact that their official currency is the U.S. Dollar probably wouldn't be high in the rhetoric.

In U.S. politics, any suggestion of annexing Mexico by force would immediately unleash the dog packs of both left and right, with the liberals howling that "We don't invade our neighbors!" and the conservatives baying "Who the hell wants it?"

The liberals would be ignoring the fact that we've invaded Canada twice and Mexico, obviously, and the conservatives would be spending too much time on what Mexico is doing now instead of looking at what it might do.

Normally, this sort of polar-opposite but mutual disavowal of reality from Congress produces some harm and certainly no good. In this case, it would be different. Getting any sort of constitutionally required Congressional approval for annexing Mexico would

require stretching the limits of stupidity, even for members of Congress, who routinely use those limits as intellectual exercise elastics.

Both sides of the congressional aisle would rightly point to the huge social and economic divides in Mexico—and the obvious and ongoing nasty problems they present—and tell any administration that proposed forced annexation that we have problems of our own, thanks, we don't need to grab lots more from somewhere else.

If we did, the foremost of those problems would be race, which would be the superscript to any other sort of problem from literacy to welfare.

In the United States, slavery, thanks to God, Abraham Lincoln and Ulysses S. Grant, is no longer a live issue. But racism, while seldom seen in public, is not yet in the grave it so richly deserves. Because of that, instant assimilation of 107 million mostly brown people would unite both white and black Americans in a single cause: "Not In My Backyard!"

Yes, that would be a sad footnote to the dream of Dr. Martin Luther King that ". . . my four little children will one day live in a nation where they will not be judged by the color of their skin but by the content of their character." But it would not, as Dr. King would quickly observe, be without precedent.

Even suggesting an acquisition of Mexico—whether by force or voluntarily –would take U.S. blacks and whites, now pretty much learning to live and let live, and unite them in a shared animosity towards their brown potential neighbors and countrymen. That venom would be reciprocated with interest from mexicanos, at least the 90 percent of them who could not blend into the Caucasian population in the U.S. or Europe.

That is, of course, racist, but anyone who truly believes that there are little or no such inklings in most people is obviously from Mars and should be deported forthwith.

We've learned to work together, live together in public places and generally be polite to one another in most venues. We've come to appreciate each other's cooking and music and fashions and fads.

But we haven't necessarily learned to *like* each other. And dropping an annexed group of 107 million "others" into that still-on-the-stove stew pot would very likely take it from simmer to boil-over. Future generations could maybe clean that stove eventually, but maybe not. And the boil-over, most suggest, would be more the competition between blacks and mexicanos at the low end of the economic scale than the competition among folks of whatever race at the high end. I mean, the well-off of any race can always smooth it over with a drink at the club, right?

Interestingly, there's some evidence to suggest that race-fueled hatred would take a back seat to economic competition.

Toward the end of May, 2006, The Christian Science Monitor published a very good story. Datelined Los Angeles and written by Daniel B. Wood, it took a look at the possible black-Latino clash over jobs.

The article outlines the feeling that Hispanics and native blacks are fighting for many of the same jobs, with the Hispanics as a whole well on their way to becoming the largest and fastest-growing minority group. It's a good piece of reporting and outlines how those in the black community both support and oppose the Hispanic wave. But the most interesting part of the article is how African –Americans view immigrants, and that is based on a Pew poll.

On the poll question "Immigrants from Latin America work very hard," the article reported that 78 percent of whites agreed and 79 percent of blacks.

Eighty-one percent of whites thought the immigrants had "strong family values" as did 77 percent of blacks.

Thirty-four percent of the whites polled by Pew, according to the article, thought immigrants from Latin America "significantly increase crime," but only

26 percent of blacks bought into that notion. Yet 37 percent of whites thought those immigrants "often go on welfare," and 33 percent of the blacks agreed.

But when asked if they or a family member had lost a job to Latino immigrants, just 14 percent of the whites agreed, but 22 percent of the blacks said yes. For the numerically challenged that means a tad above 50 percent more blacks than white in the poll had personal experience of losing a job to a Latino immigrant.

All this frames the possible friction, whether from annexation or the current *"Problem? What Problem?"* policy, not so much in racial terms as in economic terms. The Latino immigrants are viewed as hard workers with good family values. The only perceived problem is that those Latino immigrants might take a job away from me or mine.

Both *Reconquista* and *Annex Mexico* are dead letters, but they help us take a look, especially from the annexation viewpoint, of the problem eggs that would gleefully hatch. Under either scenario, here's what the United States would get, whether as the spoils of victory or the grim fodder of defeat:

Poverty. Horrible, grinding, almost inescapable poverty that sits vulture-like on the shoulders of somewhere between 40 and 50 million Mexicans who themselves, or through their family wage-earners, try to survive on between $4 and $6 US a day, depending upon whose estimate you believe. Blame it on whatever suits your politics—lack of education, lack of opportunity, lack of initiative, lack of being like you or me—the inescapable fact is that more than one out of three Mexicans have more in common with someone in equatorial Africa than they do someone (not related) in New York City, except maybe some of the homeless, most of whom scrape together more than $6 a day.

The World Bank paints an even bleaker picture. Basing its figure on 2002, it pegged half the Mexican population as poor, with one fifth of the population living in what it said was "extreme poverty." That group is primarily, but

129

not exclusively rural. Although it ac-
knowledged an upward trend, the World
Bank said 42 percent of the extremely
poor lacked access to drinking water, 74
percent lacked access to sanitation services. But 90 percent did have electricity.

The World Bank was silent on
whether it was better to be hungry and
poor in the dark or in electric light.

So annexation would take roughly 50
million persons living in various degrees
of poverty and transfer much of the
problem from Mexico City to Washington. Not the best of deals. There are
other downsides.

Racial Stew Back To Boiling. Ordinary Mexicans, for the most part, are
brown—a reflection of their Span-
ish/Amerindian primary background
with a little of African and *¿quién sabe?*
thrown in. It's a delight to the overall
goal of the human race and an awkward
moment for the current group. Americans, black, white, Latino and Asian
have achieved a workable societal formula that is essentially based upon

numbers in various social classes. It's not unlike a multi-part mobile, where the weight of each object is carefully counterbalances by the weight of all the other objects, and hence, all move in a forced harmony.

Drop more than 100 million Mexicans onto that mobile and what you get is not a mobile, but a whirlygig

This is not because Mexicans are better or worse than any other group, including Americans, but because the balance of groups with any society is worked out over time, with give and take and friction and adjustment. The last time American society saw the mass influx of people from one class to another was the emancipation of slaves at the end of the civil war. That threw things out of balance in such a way that it took 150 years before the wobbles and bumps of readjustment became manageable. Annexing Mexico would be volunteering to go through that experience again. And it can't be compared to the great waves of immigration from 1890 to 1920 and after World War II—the majority of those immigrants were Caucasian, and as soon as their kids learned native American speech and dress, they became, if they wished, indistinguishable from anyone else.

Infrastructure. Well, Mexico obviously has some. But it doesn't go everywhere. We're talking roads here, and basic water, electricity and sanitation. In the cities, at the top of the heap, *yes!* In much of the rest of the country, *no!*

We are also talking standards that differ dramatically from the U.S. norm in very many aspects of daily existence. A small example: In the U.S., the underlying assumption of connection to a public sewer system is that the waste winds up in a treatment plant. In Mexico, that may not be the case, and the "sewer system" may be nothing more than a covered conduit as opposed to an open sewer. That leads to water quality and water-borne illness rates that are multiples of those in the U.S. and even generates higher rates in the U.S. bordertown populations that share a water boundary with Mexico.

Another is telephones. They aren't in every Mexican household. The Economist's Global Technology Forum reported that Mexico's federal telecommunications commission pegged the penetration at 15.7 fixed lines per 100 people.

That works out to a shade more than half of the households. To be fair, mobile telephone penetration is running in the same ballpark. As with many U.S./ Mexican comparisons, most figures are estimates.

This estimate is from the CIA World Factbook information on communications, presented here is tabular form. The information is dated from 2004 to 2006.

Telephone Lines United States	Telephone Lines Mexico
268,0000—90 per 100 population	18,073,200—17 per 100 population
Mobile Phones United States	Mobile Phones Mexico
203,824,428— about 68% of popu-	38,451,100— about 36% of

lation	population
Internet Hosts United States	Internet Hosts Mexico
195,138,696	2,026,633
Internet Users United States	Internet Users Mexico
203,824,428—68% of population	16,995,400—16% of population

The infrastructure disparity goes well beyond water, sewage and telephones, especially in the core economic component of transportation. While it is true that cheap labor by illegal, mostly Mexican immigrants contributes a lot to putting fresh, cheap fruits and vegetables on U.S. family tables year-round, it is also true that much of the crop would rot in California, Florida and elsewhere, were it not for a magnificent network of highways, rivers, railroads and airports that move those things—and every other imaginable thing—from A to B daily. For almost all of the United States, certainly in the lower 48, the phrase "You can't get there from here" has only literary meaning.

134

In the United States, we can sing or snarl "Hit the road, Jack!" and be confident that Jack is somewhere in the vicinity of the almost 75,000 kilometers of expressways that lace the country together, not to mention the 4 million kilometers of other paved roads and just ignoring the 2.2 million kilometers of unpaved.

But if you sing "Hit the road, Juan!" the choices for Juan in Mexico are less complete. In a country with about 20 percent of the area of the United States, there are just 349,038 kilometers of roads of any description, only 6,979 kilometers of those expressways, with the total paved roads coming to 116,928 kilometers.

To highlight the economic effect of a good highway/road system, it's only necessary to look at a factoid Time magazine published in a bit about the 50th anniversary of the U.S. Interstate system. That system, it said, saves the average consumer $1,292 a year. Which is more than many Mexicans earn in a year, never mind saving on transportation costs.

The same disparity pops up no matter which form of transportation you examine. The U.S. has some 227,736 kilometers of railways, while Mexico has just 17, 634. Sure, Mexico covers a smaller area, but even assuming a railway-to-area equality, Mexico should have more than 45,000 kilometers of track.

The story continues for airports. Counting just those with paved runways, the ones most likely to help in the economy, the United States has 5,120 and Mexico has 227. To put that in perspective, Canada, with a population less than a third of Mexico's, has 508 airports with paved runways.

And to those who would counter than Canada, after Russia, is the biggest country on earth, it should be remembered that 90 percent of the Canadian population lives with 100 miles of the U.S. border.

Internal waterways—as opposed to coastlines—are an important commer-

cial highway, but they are mostly the result of Mother Nature's dice roll, and it's
unfair to use them as an infrastructure
comparison, although the lack of them
certainly doesn't help. For the record,
Mexico has just 2,900 kilometers of
navigable rivers and coastal canals,
compared with 19,312 in the United
States, which doesn't count the 3,769
kilometers of the St. Lawrence Seaway,
which is shared with Canada.

As for the coastline itself, fronting on
the Pacific, the Gulf of California, both
sides of the Gulf of Mexico, and a sliver
of the Caribbean, Mexico owns 9,330
kilometers, on which it has seven commercial ports: Altamira, Manzanillo,
Morro Redondo, Salina Cruz, Tampico,
Topolobampo and Veracruz. There it's
on a parity with the U.S., which has ten,
commercial ports if you make decisions
that say Philadelphia is an international
commercial port, but Boston isn't, and
don't count the ports on the Mississippi
or the Great Lakes, all accessible to foreign commerce.

The point of this Death By Numbers exercise is very simple. If the United States were to annex Mexico, the pressure to transform Mexico to a commercial par with the rest of the U.S. would be tremendous, and an expense beyond imagining except over centuries.

But while the vision of economists and historians may span centuries, the vision of someone who is poor mostly extends to the next possible meal. And if that doesn't happen, and others under the same government live in plenty, the result is rage and violence.

This socio-economic volcano has consumed most of Mexico now, as witnessed by the bitterly contested presidential election, with one leader, Felipe Calderón, coming from the upper-class and business backers and another, Andrés Manuel López Obrador, who also holds a university degree, portraying himself as a champion of the poor. Calderón won by a very slim margin, marked by unsurprising protests and rhetoric from his opponents. But even if all opponents and voter of the non-

Calderón persuasion had not said a word Calderón really won six years to govern Mexico with the certain knowledge that two-thirds of his countrymen very much wanted someone else in the presidential sash.

So for both the largely web-based advocates of either Reconquista or Annexation, a small consolation prize based upon your keen insights:

There's this really nifty bridge from Manhattan to Brooklyn and you, brilliant as you are, can get it for a song. . .

Jeez Louize, It Ain't Broke, So Why are We Trying To Fix It?

Mark Twain wrote "Suppose you were an idiot. And suppose you were a member of Congress. But I repeat myself." That's still pretty apt when you look at the posturing and preening in Congress today as it holds hearings and proposes bills to "deal with the border problem."

The preferred way of dealing with the border problem for members of Congress always seems to involve hearings, speeches and news conferences—or pretty much any place else where the cameras are active and Congressman Flipabird can get the limelight.

Well, horses can't help but produce their end-product and neither can Representatives and Senators, although it must be noted that Senators, being outnumbered more than four-to-one by Representatives, deserve credit for an equal share of end-product despite a smaller number of producers.

Must be experience.

So the rest of us, who must work to support these garden-friendly Congressional producers as well as ourselves, are entitled to ask about illegal, mostly Mexican immigration, "Why is this a problem and why do we have to fix it?" After all, a lot of work is being done by these immigrants and they are supporting their families and teaching solid values to their children and whenever was that thought to be a bad thing?

Work, family and values aren't bad things, but in May of 2006, Robert Rector of the Heritage Foundation, threw one hell of a skunk into the national debate garden party. Rector, a member of Washington's top conservative think

142

tank, took a novel approach to the debate: he used facts.[vi]

Rector's facts caused a panic in Congress, where an occasional pebble of fact will cause the frog pond to ripple, but a boulder of fact is a catastrophe. You can (and should) read the whole report at www.heritage.org, but here's an overview of this most comprehensive answer of why doing nothing here—meaning the current efforts in Congress—ain't gonna work.

As Rector notes, the plan proposed by Republican Senators Mel Martínez of Florida and Chuck Hagel of Nebraska, opens a gate to amnesty and eventual citizenship to illegal immigrants. Rector uses the number 9 to 10 million, but as we've said, this is more complicated than counting the packages of Twinkies shipped and numbers in this issue will differ. Nonetheless, Rector points out that when an illegal get amnesty and becomes a citizen, that person has a right to bring his or her parents here—and they may become citizens after time. Before we get all teary-eyed about the flow into the "melting pot," which we've already examined as bogus, let's look at the price tag: Rector pegs it at $30 billion per year and observes that it "would be the largest expansion of the welfare state in 35 years."

Rector was writing on May 12, 2006 and the Senate would pass the Let Them Stay bill on May 25th. The Throw Them Out bill from the House had a much different focus, and any significant compromise between the two positions was doomed to be difficult. And intended by both sides to be just that. Difficulty in compromising is an earmark of Legislation for Posturing, as opposed to Legislation for Progress.

But Rector doesn't posture or set up straw men. Rector points out that means-tested welfare use draws immigrants of whatever source, fed primarily by lower education levels for many, and hence lower earning power in American society.

After a long, skilled walk through the statistical garden, Rector's points seem to boil down to these:

- Granting amnesty to illegal immigrants will cost us big time in social services and other, less visible costs. These are traceable to lower education levels, higher crime rates and adoption of an American-Hispanic culture that holds welfare much more acceptable

- Amnesty would spur more immigration, both from the reprieved bringing their families over and from those who hadn't tried to cross the border illegally seeing the benefit conferred upon those who did and saying, in effect, me too!

Having nicely documented the problem, Rector then proposed five specific common-sense policies that government ought to follow. And there, of course, his ship ran aground—not because they aren't sound policies, but because the likelihood of this or any other government actually implementing them is very, very remote. First, from the Heritage.org web site, the five policy suggestions verbatim in bold type:[vii]

1. The influx of illegal immigrants should be stopped by rigorous border security programs and strong programs to prevent employers from employing illegals.

2. Amnesty and citizenship should not be given to current illegal immigrants. Amnesty has negative fiscal consequences and is manifestly unfair to those who have waited for years to enter the country lawfully. Amnesty would also serve as a magnet, drawing even more future illegal immigration.

3. Any guest worker program should grant temporary, not permanent, residence and should not be a pathway to citizenship. A guest worker program should not disproportionately swell the ranks of low-skill workers.

4. Children born to parents who are illegal immigrants or to future guest workers should not be given citizenship status. Granting citizenship automatically confers welfare eligibility and makes it unlikely the parent will ever leave the U.S.

5. The legal immigration system grants lawful permanent residence to some 950,000 persons each year. This system should be altered to substantially increase the proportion of new entrants with high levels of education and skills in demand by U.S. firms. Under current law, foreign-born parents and siblings of naturalized citizens are given preference for entry visas. The current visa allotments for family members (other than spouses and minor children) should be eliminated, and quotas for employment and skill-based entry, increased proportionately.

Those are intelligent principles based on a sound analysis, which means that although Congress twittered at this rude introduction of fact into debate, the chances of those principles being followed are about those of a chicken in the fox coop.

Politics in the beginning of the 21st century is not so much the art of the possible as the reign of the probable. So here are probable legislative reactions, by the numbers to Rector's good sense:

1. *"Rigorous border security" costs big bucks, but doesn't necessarily generate big votes, and, in fact, will really honk off most of my major contributors who depend on Juan Nodocumenta to make a living. Besides which, I flunked Lawnmower 101.*

2. *You're absolutely right, pal, but lemme tell ya. Life is unfair. And, as you have highlighted, government is inept. If we were organized enough to find and deport them, they*

wouldn't have gotten here in the first place.

3. *Like we said, we're no good at keeping track of anyone to begin with. And as far as limiting guest workers to highly-skilled folk, thanks for the opportunity to portray you as an anti-Little Guy type. It'll help me paint myself as for the Little Guy (as long as he happens to be me).*

4. *Saying something like this in public, however much sense it makes, would make me the target of a Joint Liberal/Conservative Lynch Mob, who would both thunder that I shouldn't be visiting the sins of the fathers and mothers on their children while they knotted the noose and looked for a tree.*

5. *Maybe you want to be presented to an electorate as the guy who said Granny couldn't come to the States and live out her life, surrounded by*

149

*her family, but I gotta tell you, guy, I
don't.*

This probable legislative reaction to
what are very sensible proposals reflects
two of the great truths of political life.
(1.) If It Ain't Broke, Don't Fix It and (2.)
It ain't broke until I say it is." Anyone
who doubts that should review the poli-
ticking over the U.S. Social Security System.

Both of those truths reflect things
we've touched on before. Illegal immigrants, whether from Mexico or elsewhere, wouldn't come here if there was
no work. And there wouldn't be work if
those of us who are here didn't offer it to
them.

In that sense, most of us are break-
ing the law fully as much as the illegal
immigrants. In 2005, I had my house
painted and a thousand-gallon oil tank
removed from the driveway. In 2006, I
had that driveway redone. In all cases,
only the foreman of the crew who came
by at the beginning and end of the job
day spoke English.

Well, although I wasn't their direct employer, didn't I demand documentation?

Hell no.

I gave cold drinks and lawn chairs in the shade for breaks and all three crews gave me outstanding work.

Legal or not, I think it's called capitalism. You know, finding a need and filling it for a profit at a price folks will pay. That's what's happening now with illegal immigration, and the folks who want to put a death ray along the border should remember that the last time the government tried to impose a widely unpopular behavior on the American people, it was called Prohibition.

Prohibition didn't reduce drinking. It did give a tremendous boost to organized crime, which supplied a need at a fair price. Sure, the mob settled disputes by extremely binding arbitration, but it wouldn't have existed if there weren't customers for its services. Or as the archetypical Chicago gangster Al Capone once explained, *"When I sell liquor, it's called bootlegging; when my patrons serve it on Lake Shore Drive, it's called hospitality."*

If, by some magic federal wand, all illegal immigrants were to disappear tomorrow morning, there would be criminal activity to bring them back—for a fee, of course—by tomorrow evening.

And most of them would be from Mexico, with the majority of the rest passing through Mexico.

If there were no demand for the jobs illegal immigrants do in the United States of America, there would be few illegal immigrants. If you are starving, humping hundreds of miles to merely starve somewhere else isn't under consideration. But although we can complain that they live here in squalid conditions and work under the same conditions, they do send home that $20 billion US a year and have lives that are better than they had in their home countries.

Americans of all peoples should understand that the tide of human opportunity is not something that mere governments can turn. People everywhere want a better life, and the enterprising among them are willing to do whatever it takes—legal or not—to get it and pass it on to their children.

We said as much in our own Declaration of Independence, which, be reminded, was treasonously illegal in the then-current law of the American colonies.

We saw as much when the Soviet Union collapsed, the Berlin Wall fell and Maoist Communist China started to become the Final Frontier of consumerism. And now we're seeing it in the flood of illegal, mostly Mexican, immigrants who actually don't want to leave their home countries, but aren't interested in starving to death there either. Or permanently abandoning their families. Or condemning their children to the same fate.

The fact that is conveniently overlooked in all the hoohaw about illegal immigration is that these folks are doing exactly what we teach our kids is the American dream: they're making their own way, pulling themselves up by bootstraps and hard work and trying to make a better life for themselves today and their children tomorrow.

To be against that is truly un-American, and we have to find a way beyond the nonsense of fences and armed patrols to recognize the realities of North America in the 21st century.

Alright, Wise Guy–Now what?

The answer to the problem of Mexican illegal immigration was developed in 1986 in some islands in the Pacific Ocean. As a nation, we just haven't been bright enough to bring it ashore. Some history.

In World War II, we fought Germany and Italy on the continent of Europe, but we fought Japan on islands spread all across the Pacific. Prior to the war, Japan had seized and fortified many islands, judging quite correctly that they were unsinkable aircraft carriers and fueling stations.

Unsinkable, yes, but not impregnable. The stepping stones Imperial Japan used to expand its empire became the stepping stones the allies would use to disband it.

When Hiroshima and Nagasaki ended one age of horror and ushered in another, the islands became something of a problem for the fledgling United Nations. For many islands, handing them back to the Japanese wasn't in the cards, and their previous overseers, the Germans, weren't good candidates either.

So the United Nations, even at that nascent stage, did what it would do many times, which was to flip the problem to the United States, creating the Trust Territory of the Pacific Islands. The United States Navy ran the show from 1947 to 1951 and then turned it over to the United States Department of the Interior, although the islands were about as far from the U.S. interior as you could get, and then, as now, the primary economic engines were subsistence farming and fishing.

Eventually, by 1986, the Trust Territory of the Pacific Islands got carved into three sovereign states, the Federated

States of Micronesia (FSM) the Republic of the Marshall Islands (RMI) and the Republic of Palau. These are not major world-stage players. The Federated States of Micronesia's population as of July 2006 was estimated at 108,000—less than half the number of folk who daily commute between New Jersey and Manhattan on the PATH trains.

The interesting thing about all this is that these three sovereign nations are voluntarily associated with the United States under agreements called Compact of Free Association. For FSM and RMI, the compacts were ratified in 1986 and were extended for another 20 years in 2004. The compact with the Republic of Palau's compact was effective in 1995 and ends in 2009, unless renegotiated.

The FSM and RMI compacts are lengthy and wordy, running more than 280 pages when kept in Adobe's .pdf format, and anyone who reads it from end to end certainly deserves a medal, as well as the chance to get a life. But it's the essentials that are attractive to the Mexico illegal immigration issue.

157

First, the United States is responsible for the defense of these three sovereign states. They are free to make treaties, have embassies, establish their own laws, what have you, but if some neighbor gets grabby, it will find itself staring at the United States Marine Corps, which will not be amused.

Second, the United States provides economic aid, important to tiny specks of coral and rock that are too remote to draw tourism and have few resources other than the sea.

But third, and this is the kicker, the citizens of these three states "...may reside, travel and work in the United States without restriction." That's a quote from those gimlet-eyed folk at the IRS, whose interest in who's working here and under what rules is obvious.

So yes, it's one hell of a canoe paddle from the islands with a Compact of Free Association agreement even to the closest American state, Hawaii, but if a citizen of one of those republics shows a valid passport, and isn't a felon or other generally unwanted type, they can enter the U.S.

Beyond the right of entry, and the services of the Armed Forces of The United States, the folk on those tiny islands in the Pacific get several billion dollars a year of aid, not because Uncle Sam is just a swell fella, but because, as Dana R. Dillon of the Heritage Foundation pointed out when the compacts of two of the three were up for renewal in 2003, what the state in the compact offer is location, location, location. Meaning:

We deny the 500,000 square miles of the Pacific between Guam and Hawaii to foreign military. The last time foreign military got a hold there, we called it World War II.

Kwajalein in the Marshal Islands is the only site in the world for full-scale testing of long-range missiles. And it's also handy for missile defense.

The area is very handy for eavesdropping on folks who may not love us and is a support point for the space program.

159

Well, that's nifty, but whatever does it have to do with the illegal immigration problem coming from Mexico?

In a word, everything.

It provides a framework for the meeting the real needs of Mexico's poor and U.S. labor demand without disturbing the economy or sovereignty of either Mexico or the United States. It provides a framework for recognizing reality, something not common in international diplomacy, but not without precedent. And it provides a framework for moving forward, which may not be as much fun for politicians on both sides of the border as meaningless chest-beating, but is closer to what their fellow citizens pay them to do.

We are also in a moment of rare opportunity. On December 1, 2006, with the presidential sash of responsibility assumed by Felipe Calderon, the one-term six-year window of potential accomplishment yawns wide, looking out over a country so deeply divided by class and wealth that it absolutely needs the safety valve of U.S. immigration, legal or not.

George W. Bush, past the last mid-term elections of his presidency, looks for a legacy more enduring than probably ephemeral regime changes in Afghanistan and Iraq. Real immigration reform bills from the House and the Senate that are far apart on everything except the zero probability of passage.

And the United States looks at the de facto start of its next presidential election, an unusual one in that neither eventual candidate will be shoveling discourse from the vice presidential box.

It all means that existing executive leadership can do the right thing as they see it without worrying a lot about political consequences to themselves and their parties if it later turns out to have been the wrong thing.

But what really puts the Gold Seal on this moment of rare opportunity is that the time when we could ignore the problem and pass it on to the future is firmly in the past. The governments of both the United States of Mexico and the United

States of America must seize the immigration issue or it will surely seize them. We often speak of Mexico's need for a safety valve for the half of its population that is desperately poor. We speak much less often of the United States need for the labor of immigrants, illegal or not but mostly Mexican or via Mexico. Mayor Michael Bloomberg of New York City is hardly anti-business, and not given to wild flights of rhetoric (or, for that matter, wild flights of anything.) But he put an intelligent position on the issue succinctly in his testimony to the Senate Judiciary Committee holding field hearing on immigration.

On July 5, 2006 in Philadelphia, part of Bloomberg's prepared text said this:

"Immigration reform is one of the most important issues this Congress faces, and no city will be more affected by the outcome of the debate than New York. To begin, let me say how appropriate it is that this hearing is taking place here in Philadelphia.

"Two hundred and thirty years ago yesterday, just around the corner from here, our founding fathers adopted the greatest statement on the right to self-government ever written. Among those who signed the Declaration of Independence were nine immigrants, and at every other crucial stage in American history— from ratification of the Constitution to the Civil War to the Industrial Revolution to the computer age -- immigrants have propelled America to greatness.

"Today, we remain a nation of immigrants. People from around the world continue to come here seeking opportunity, and they continue to make America the most dynamic nation in the world. But it's clear we also have a problem on our hands -- our immigration laws are fundamentally broken.

"It's as if we expect border control agents to do what a century of communism could not: defeat the natural market forces of supply and demand and defeat the natural human desire for freedom and opportunity. You might as well sit in

163

your beach chair and tell the tide not to come in.

"As long as America remains a nation dedicated to the proposition that 'all men are created equal, endowed by their Creator with certain unalienable Rights, that among these are Life, Liberty and the pursuit of Happiness,' people from near and far will continue to seek entry into our country.

"New York City alone—is home to more than three million immigrants, who make up nearly 40 percent of our entire population. About 500,000 came to our City—and continue to come illegally.

"And let's be honest: they arrive for a good reason—they want a better life for themselves and their families, and our businesses need them and hire them!

"Although they broke the law by illegally crossing our borders or overstaying their visas, and our businesses broke the law by employing them. our City's economy would be a shell of itself had they not, and it would collapse if they were deported. The same holds true for the nation.

164

"For our children to have a bright future, two things are true: a strong America needs a constant source of new immigrants. And in a post 9/11 world, a secure America needs to make sure that those immigrants arrive here legally.

"We have a right—and a duty—to encourage people to come, and at the same time, to ensure that no one who is on a terrorist watch list sneaks into our country. Right now, we neither invite those we want, nor keep out those we don't. If we are going to both strengthen our national security and keep our economy growing, you -- our elected legislators—must devise a comprehensive approach to immigration reform.

"I believe that such an approach must embody four key principles: 1) reducing incentives; 2) creating more lawful opportunity; 3) reducing illegal access; and 4) accepting reality. Allow me to briefly outline each of them.

"First, we must reduce the incentive to come here illegally. As a business owner, I know the absurdity of our existing immigration regulations all too well. Em-

ployers are required to check the status of all job applicants, but not to do anything more than eyeball their documents. In fact, hypocritically, under Federal law that Congress wrote, employers are not even permitted to ask probing questions. As a result, fake 'Green cards' are a dime a dozen—you can buy one for 40 bucks. Fake Social Security cards are also easily obtained. And for $50 cash, you can get both cards. Such a deal!

"As most members of the U.S. Senate recognize, we absolutely must have a Federal database that will allow employers to verify the status of all job applicants. But for this database to have any value, we must also ensure that the documentation job applicants present is incorruptible. That means we need to create a bio-metric employment card containing unique information—fingerprints or DNA, for instance.

"Every current job holder or applicant would be required to obtain a card, and every business would be required to check its validity against the Federal database. In theory, we already have such a card—it's called your Social Security card. But being a government product, naturally, its technology is way behind the times.

"By taking advantage of current technology, we can provide the Federal government with the tools necessary to enforce our immigration laws and protect workers from exploitative and abusive conditions. I want to be clear that this is not a national ID card, as some have suggested. This would be an employment card for the 21st Century. If you don't work, you don't need a card. But everyone who works would need to have an employment card.

"There must also be stiff penalties for businesses that fail to conduct checks or ignore their results.

"Holding businesses accountable is the crucial step, because it is the only way to reduce the incentive to come here illegally. Requiring employers to verify citizenship status was the promise of the 1986 immigration reform law. But it was an empty promise, never enforced by the Federal government.

"The failure to enforce the law was largely in response to pressure from businesses—which is understandable, because businesses needed access to a larger labor supply than Federal immigration laws allowed.

"Apparently, fixing that problem by increasing legal immigration, as opposed to looking the other way on illegal immigration, was never seriously considered by Congress, until very recently. Instead, by winking at businesses that hired illegal immigrants, the Federal government sent a clear signal to those in other countries: If you can make it into our country, you'll have no trouble qualifying for employment.

"And so—it's no surprise—people have been coming at such high levels that our border control simply cannot stop them. Unless we reduce the incentive to come here illegally, increasing our Border Patrol will have little impact on the number of people who enter illegally. We will waste the money spent, jeopardize lives, and deceive the public with a false prom-

ise of security that Congress knows it can't deliver.

"Second, we must increase lawful opportunity for overseas workers. Science, medicine, education, and modern industries today are all growing faster overseas than here in the U.S., reversing the century long advantage we've enjoyed. Baby boomers are starting to retire, America's birthrate continues to slow, and we don't have enough workers to pay for our retirement benefits. The economics are very simple: We need more workers than we have.

"That means we must increase the number of visas for overseas manual workers, who help provide the essential muscle and elbow grease we need to keep our economy running. It also means we must increase the number of visas for immigrant engineers, doctors, scientists, and other professionally trained workers -- the innovators of tomorrow's economy. And we must give all of them, as well as foreign students, the opportunity to earn permanent status, so they can put their knowledge and entrepreneurial spirit to use for our country.

"Why shouldn't we reap the benefits of the skills foreign students have obtained here? If we don't allow them in, or we force them to go home, we will be sending the future of science -- and the jobs of tomorrow -- with them.

"Recent studies put the lie to the old argument that immigrants take jobs away from native-born Americans and significantly depress wages. Quite the contrary—they are what make our economy work. In most cases, those here illegally are filling low-wage, low-skill jobs that Americans do not want.

"Global economic forces are responsible for the declines in the real wages of unskilled workers and occur regardless of whether immigrants are present in a community. Moreover, the total economic effect of any slight wage decline produced by immigration is more than offset by substantial increases in productivity.

"To keep people and businesses investing in America, we need to ensure that we have workers for all types of jobs.

170

"Third, we must reduce illegal access to our borders, which, as I've said, is a matter of urgent national security. As President Bush recognizes, in some areas, particularly in border towns, additional fencing may be required; in open desert areas, a virtual wall, created through sensors and cameras, will be far more effective.

"However, even after we double the number of border agents, they will remain overwhelmed by the flood of people attempting to enter illegally. Only by embracing the first two principles -- reducing incentives and increasing lawful opportunity -- will border security become a manageable task.

"Members of the House of Representatives want to control the borders. So do all of us here. But believing that increasing border patrols alone will achieve that goal is either naïve and short-sighted, or cynical and duplicitous. No wall or army can stop hundreds of thousands of people each year.

"Fourth, and finally, we need to get real about the people who are now living

in this country illegally, in many cases raising families and paying taxes. The idea of deporting these 11 or 12 million people -- about as many as live in the entire state of Pennsylvania– is pure fantasy. Even if we wanted to, it would be physically impossible to carry out. If we attempted it, and it would be perhaps the largest round-up and deportation in world history, the social and economic consequences would be devastating.

"Let me ask you: Would we really want to spend billions of dollars on a round-up and deportation program that would split families in two, only to have these very same people and millions more, illegally enter our country again? Of course not. America is better than that—and smarter than that.

"That's why I do not believe that the American people will support the short-sighted approach to this issue taken by the House, which would make felons of illegal immigrants.

"The Senate's tiered-approach, however, is flawed, too. Requiring some people to 'report to deport' through guest *worker programs, while leaving their spouses, children, and mortgages behind, is no less naïve than thinking we can deport 12 million people. What incentive would people have to show up?*

"In fact, this approach would just create an enormous incentive for fraud, and there can be little doubt that the black market for false documentation would remain strong and real enforcement impossible. If we're going to create a market for deceit, why not have Uncle Sam sell the fake papers, so we can at least get paid for it? It would be absurd, of course, but no less so than expecting people to line up for deportation.

"There is only one practical solution, and it is a solution that respects the history of our nation: Offer those already here the opportunity to earn permanent status and keep their families together.

"For decades, the Federal government has tacitly welcomed them into the workforce, collected their income and Social Security taxes, which about two-thirds of undocumented workers pay, and bene-

fited immeasurably from their contributions to our country.

"Now, instead of pointing fingers about the past, let's accept the present for what it is by bringing people out of the shadows, and focus on the future by casting those shadows aside, permanently.

"As the debate continues between the House and Senate, I urge members of Congress to move past the superficial debate over the definition of 'amnesty.' Buzz words and polls should not dictate national policies.

"We need Congress to lead from the front, not the back, and that means adopting a solution that is enforceable, sustainable, and compassionate -- and that enables the American economy to thrive in the 21st century. Perhaps now more than ever before, it's time to vote for our future, and not pander to parochial fears." [viii]

The mayor went on to kvetch about Homeland Security money—hey, that's what he's paid to do—but his words on the Mexican illegal immigration problem are sensible, honest and eloquent.

We can no longer ignore the issue, but we can seize it if the United States and Mexico do it together, and so forge an alliance of admiration and mutual accommodation out of one increasingly marked by animosity.

Yeah, well, How do we do that?

The first thing, and always the toughest thing, is to admit that there must be a change. For all the revolutionary rhetoric, most politicians have an absolute interest in the status quo. After all, that's how they got where they are, and any radical change of that scene risks putting them out looking for jobs like the rest of us. Which is how most politicians define unacceptable risk.

But suppose that Tinkerbell, who has long since joined the National Organization of Women and filed multiple harassment lawsuits against Peter Pan and the Lost Boys, decides to do North America a favor and sprinkle her pixie dust on Mexico City and Washington? Then, enabled magically to fly above their dirt-bound visions of self-interest, political leaders of Mexico and the United States might do something like this.

First, the presidents of Mexico and the United States would announce that both countries were tired of playing make-believe about the borders, and that they, as well as anyone with even a bit of humanity, would no longer support any program that would disrupt families and kill innocents in the desert whose only "crime" was that they wanted to find work so they could eat and help their folks back home do the same.

Then, each president would appoint two negotiators. From the American side, the Former Presidential Odd Couple of George H.W. Bush and Bill Clinton come to mind. No, they don't see eye to eye on a lot of stuff, but as former presidents and staunch patriots, they have the national interest firmly at heart, right next to their obligation as human beings. And their own credibility with their part of the two main political parties in the United States is unmatched.

From the Mexican side, Vicente Fox and Andrés Manuel López Obrador, when the latter finally stops whining and resumes working. Neither of them is bound to the PRI's seven decades of rule, both have an interest in preventing a cataclysmic split in Mexico's social order, and both agree that coming to some sort of agreement with the United States makes sense. And the credibility of each with the two main parts of Mexico's potentially explosive economic divide is unmatched.

The most important thing is that whoever is chosen on either side must have Kevlar immunity from being micromanaged, whether by their respective Congresses, presidential staffs or the presidents who appointed them themselves. Sure, they should have general marching orders, agreed to by both chief executives. But after that, the presidents of the United States and Mexico should go find babies to kiss. Negotiating between heads of state, or between obvious puppets of heads of state doesn't work. And this one needs to work.

So what should the joint marching orders given to the distinguished negotiators look like?

The first and foremost order should be to keep their mouths shut about the negotiations, except to their own governments, and then only when a situation not within the bounds of the general marching orders develops. Leaks and trial balloons will do nothing more productive than cause massive yapping in the press kennels of both Mexico and the United States. Negotiations, like sex, proceed with greater ease and productivity in private. So discourse with the press should be limited to a smile, wave and appropriate seasonal greeting.

The second order should be that these negotiations must produce a suggested agreement that all the negotiators can endorse. The illegal immigration problem in the United States and the twin problem of enduring poverty for many in Mexico are far too important and serious to be hindered by the 'gotcha!' instinct of ordinary diplomacy. This is not about some obscure treaty provision, but about the lives and futures of tens of millions today, and by extension, the almost half-billion souls in both countries tomorrow.

All that said, if Tinkerbell does her work and this starts to happen, here are points that should be on the agenda.

Defense Obligations.

Mexico spends a far smaller percentage of its budget on the military, and has the smallest number of military personnel per capita of any country in Latin America. That is because Mexico's leaders have figured out that they really aren't part of Latin America for defense purposes, just as they aren't part of South America for geographic purposes. Since World War II and the emergence of the United States as first a superpower, and then, the Last Superpower Standing, Mexico's defense against major foreign aggression has been a phone call to Washington.

181

Any foreign power thinking of messing with Mexico over the last 60 years has had to factor in that they would soon be looking down the gun barrels of the United States Army, Navy, Air Force and Marine Corps—and really, really wishing they weren't. As the United States demonstrated in Grenada and Panama in the 1980s, there is a limit to the things we will tolerate in our backyard, and when that limit is reached, the consequences will be swift and final. Mexico is our next-door neighbor, which sets U.S. tolerance for hassling Mexico very, very low.

This is *not* to say that the members of Mexico's Armed Forces wouldn't defend their country with honor and bravery and skill. It is to say, however, that they simply are equipped and trained for a different mission—domestic civil order and disaster relief—and that they shouldn't be asked to do more although they would try bravely. A U.S. Navy carrier battle group easily overwhelms the entire armed forces of Mexico in equipment, logistics and the ability to project lethal force. We have twelve such groups, more on the way.

If, under a Compact of Free Association, Mexico and the United States recognize the de facto responsibility of the United States for Mexico's defense against foreign aggression, both countries win.

Mexico wins the freedom to focus its existing military, and a portion of its existing military spending, on ending the grinding poverty that is the hallmark of the southern half of Mexico. Subcomandante Marcos and his Zapatista buddies would find something else to do if Mexico City was truly providing the services, education and seed money so desperately needed. And labor and organization. A member of Mexico's armed forces who brings electricity and clean water to a poor village in Southern Mexico has defended his country with honor equal to repulsing a foreign foe.

The United States Wins the right to expand our defensive perimeter all the way south down to Guatemala and Belize, making illegal or hostile entry from either the Pacific or Gulf of Mexico more difficult, and solidifying the Gulf of Mexico into a de facto Mexican-American Lake.

Topics for discussion: It would probably be a good idea for a large United States Navy installation, including air station, to be built somewhere around Salina Cruz, southeast of Oaxaca. That gives quick Pacific access more than a thousand miles south of San Diego, and brings the local economic boost that invariably accompanies a permanent U.S. military base to an area that needs it.

Yes, there would be political protests and maybe even terrorist attacks over the "Yanqui Occupation," but experience around the world shows that the only thing that frets many locals more than a huge military presence in their neighborhoods is the possibility that it will go away and take with it the many millions of dollars pumped into the immediate local economy.

Both sides would have to develop a mechanism for working through the kinks. Suppose, for example, that sovereign Mexico decides it's fine for North Korea to send a ship to Puerto Vallarta, even while Washington wouldn't let that ship anywhere near U.S. territory? How should the skipper of a U.S. guided missile cruiser 20 miles off the Mexican coast it is defending react? And to which capital should he or she look for orders? Those are not easy questions, but they aren't insurmountable ones either. Look at the decades-long success of NORAD, the joint U.S.-Canadian missile early warning system that kept a nightlight burning through the darkest times of the Cold War. The commander, and hence all staff, are directly responsible to the President of the United States and the Prime Minister of Canada. NORAD worked and is working. This could too.

Free Movement Obligations

For little kids and their moms and dads to have to risk their lives in the incredibly harsh deserts of the U.S./Mexican border so that daddy can get a job painting houses and finally

185

earn enough to feed his family is obscene.

There is no other way to describe it. Those who wrap themselves in the "it's illegal!" mantle should ask themselves if they would feel comfortable taking an unwanted Thanksgiving turkey and fixings and throwing it into the disposal in front of a hungry family. If they say, "Why yes, that wouldn't bother me, after all it's ours," it is they who should be in the disposal.

All that said, we still must have reasonable control of our borders, so what's a way to do that and still have a right to be called human?

Our Compact of Free Association with our good friends in Micronesia offers some guidance. We'll talk of the Republic of the Marshall Islands and the Federated States of Micronesia, because their agreements are different in details from that with the Republic of Palau, and because they represent a majority of the populations.

Simply put, if someone from the Marshall Island or Micronesia wants to come

186

and live, study or work in the United States—and they have a valid passport from their home country—they can do so without a visa, providing they have no criminal convictions or any of the other conditions that bar admission to the U.S. And they can bring their wife and family, again with some restrictions like the kids being unmarried and under 21 years of age.

According to the U.S. Citizenship and Immigration Services Department, there are other rules for special circumstances, adoption for example, but in general, we'll give them a Form I-94, an Arrival/Departure Card, marked to show that they can stay as long as they want. They can take that passport and that card and get a valid Social Security card, and with that, they may be employed legally in the United States. For as long as they want to or need to be so employed.

If they commit a felony or become a public charge, they can be deported. They do not by this patch become permanent legal residents, aka "green card" holders and if they want to pursue

American citizenship they must first seek permanent resident status and eventually citizenship though the usual channels.

But they are not, as the mostly Mexican illegals living here now, condemned to the shadows. If someone hurts them, they can call a cop. If someone cheats them, as shamefully happened in the Katrina rebuilding, they can complain to the authorities and expect results.

So let's see, if we have somewhere between ten and twelve million Mexicans here, most illegally, trying to make enough money to live and send some home to support their relatives, but not necessarily interested in permanent residence or citizenship is this a model we might investigate?

Ya think?

Topics for discussion: We would have to work out some way for the Mexicans who are here now and don't have valid Mexican passports to get one. As has been said many times by persons of common sense, including the President of the United States and the Mayor of

New York City, sending millions of folks back home to "tag up" before they can move back to the United States is just plain dumb.

The actual logistics shouldn't be all that tough. The United States already has a passport-issuing mechanism in place, now run through local post offices. If these one-flavor ice cream shops could offer another flavor, given suitable guarantees satisfactory to both the U.S. and Mexico, there's no good reason they couldn't be the delivery vehicle. The resulting documents would still be Mexican passports and Mexico would have the sole and indisputable say on whether or not the document should be issued. But if Mexico decided ¡Sí! on an application, there is no reason why the actual document couldn't be printed and delivered in the United States.

The fate of illegal immigrants who came from other parts of Latin America, whether through Mexico or by other means, doesn't lend itself to this solution for obvious reasons. But if we ignore the overwhelming majority of the problem because we can't solve the whole problem at a stroke, then we are dumber than God intended us to be and should take remedial measures or run for Congress.

Immigration critics will certainly yell if we make it so that immigrants, mostly Mexican, must no longer flinch when they see a black-and-white police cruiser roll by, that they will have children and those children will need to be educated in public schools at taxpayer expense.

As we've said, they're already having children. Must be something about living with freedom and opportunity that makes the "not tonight, honey" bit less flippable. Besides which, the overwhelming majority of public schools in the United States are supported by property taxes, and whether you are paying rent or paying a mortgage, you're paying your share of your kids learning their ABCs.

They will do this in English eventually, bilingual programs aside. It's kind of like assimilating, but don't tell the anti-immigrant crowd that; it will deprive them of a favorite demon and they love their demons.

Social Security Obligations

The United States has agreements with 21 countries to coordinate Social Security programs so citizens of Country A working in Country B don't pay a social security tax to both countries. Makes sense.

We've had one with Canada, our neighbor to the north, since 1984. We've had one with Finland since 1992 and Luxembourg since 1993, neither exactly our close neighbors, but hey, *"I'd like to buy the world a Coke. . ."*

But we don't have one with our neighbor to the south, ten percent of whose citizens are here and working, with many paying Social Security taxes to the United States and, in theory, to Mexico.

¿Porqué?

Well, because the Social Security systems of both the United States and Mexico aren't in the best of long-term shape, and because President Bush has been sitting on an agreement hammered out in 2004 between negotiators for both countries until after the November 2006 elections.

Plenty of reason to fiddle-faddle that way, at least politically. Social Security, even when it's limited to strict domestic discourse, is a political lightning rod and a favorite ammunition of elected demagogues in need of steady pay, if not actual employment.

The key here and in any other sort of agreement about non-US social security systems is that this is an issue for accountants and actuaries, not politicians. Politically, most governments of what used to be called the West have agreed with their citizens that old age should not be a time of deprivation and that government has an obligation to do what it can to prevent that.

Demagogues who shout that an agreement with Mexico would send billions of dollars south that should rightfully go to native Americans are ignoring the many years Mexicans paid US social security taxes without hope of benefit. Or maybe they aren't aware that they've been robbing immigrants and having promised the money elsewhere, they're loathe to give it back.

Topics for discussion: Mexican and American social security withholding rates for both employee and employer are different and the systems have different reaches and goals in their home societies. The challenge facing negotiators of a compact of Free Association with Mexico will be to make the conjoined systems work so that retirement in one's home country would be identical to the retirement of one who had never left it. If Juan Cerveza and Joe Sixpack work side by side in the U.S. for 25 years and retire, Juan to Mexico and Joe to Florida, and Juan winds up getting a bigger retirement check each month than Joe, this is not going to sit too well with the Sixpack family, and rightfully so.

Working that out will not be a simple task, and may not be resolved on a first round of negotiations, or even a tenth.

But if the commission of patriots from Mexico and the United States keeps in mind that almost any beginning will be a significant victory, it need not block the path towards a solution. In fact, find the solution would not be so much the goal of the suggested commission as the resolve to set off on the path toward it together, with those setting the pace of the march being the accountants and actuaries.

In that sense, Mexico and the United States and every other developed or developing country face the same problem. Their older citizens, most inconveniently, are failing to die, while their younger citizens are failing to make enough babies. This inevitably leads to fewer and fewer supporting the more and more, which is the classic recipe for Pop Tart A La Something's Gotta Give.

That is not the problem we seek to address here. And we are all reminded that Mexican and United States negotiators crafted an agreement on Social Security they thought a decent and workable first step back in 2004. It must still be approved by the president, and then Congress has 60 days to say yes or no, which is 180 degrees opposite of the procedure outlined in the U.S. Constitution, so maybe chucking that whole thing and reincorporating it in a Compact of Free Association could restart the process and bring it to a better end.

Health Insurance, Vaccinations

Mexico wraps its version of national health in its social security plan, and the United States is still deciding whether it wants to extend its de facto national health care system (Medicare and Medicaid) to the general population, but the problem comes when an uninsured alien, legal or not, needs urgent medical care.

Laws in the United States say that hospitals which refuse emergency care because of lack of insurance or other source of funds for payment invite scores of regulators and government attorneys to perform an indefinite flamenco on their corporate skulls, charging handsomely all the while, which is why hospitals will treat those folk. (The actual law is called the Emergency Medical Treatment and Active Labor Act—EMTALA.)

If we buy the general number that 40 million persons in the United States have no, or inadequate, medical insurance, and figure that the 10-12 million of those folk are probably illegals, it's not hard to deduce that American taxpayers are picking up a good sized tab that belongs mostly to Mexico.

Since the figures, where available, are kept by states, and since the federal government picks up part of the tab but doesn't necessarily sort it from other Medi-whatever data, a good figure is hard to find. In California, the generally accepted uninsured/underinsured yearly tab to state taxpayers is around $1 billion a year.

California is thought to host roughly 40 percent of the nation's illegal immigrants, so if we assume that the California group cost the federal government another $1 billion, we can extrapolate

196

the national uninsured illegal alien medical tab at $5 billion a year.

There are higher estimates and lower, but what the negotiators for a Compact of Free Association should focus on are two relatively simple points:

No one in need of medical assistance should be denied help. Never. Ever. If we fail to understand and act upon that, we should initiate reverse evolution and go back to being plains apes so the dolphins can have a shot at developing intelligence—and doing a better job of it.

Somebody besides state and local governments in the United States has got to pick up the tab for illegals.

Topics for discussion: It ought not to be too hard to work out a system under a Compact of Free Association whereby the Mexican Government would pay for the medical treatment given to its uninsured passport-bearing citizens working and living in the United States. If a provision to that effect could be hammered into a Compact of Free Association, the "medical care to uninsured illegals" problem would largely vanish because:

197

They wouldn't be uninsured; they'd be backed by the full faith and credit of the United States of Mexico's trillion-dollar-and growing economy, one to which they are already contributing nicely by shipping money home.

They wouldn't be illegal; they would be in this country with the full permission of Mexico and the United States with a passport and entry form to prove it.

Would there be thousands of rules and details and forms to be devised and inaugurated? Yeah, but the simplicity of getting and paying for medical care has been declining since the norm was paying a dead chicken to the witch doctor for a spell. Since then the quality of the treatment has improved mightily; the quality of the payment plan has not.

Another point for discussion would be required vaccinations.

Babies born in the United States spend the first few years of their lives convinced they are being trained as pincushions. What used to be the traditional diseases of childhood have long

198

since met their end at needlepoint, as well as the killer diseases of smallpox and polio and many of the annoyances, or threats, of adulthood. That is the same for babies born here to immigrants illegal or not. Don't forget that the kid's legal in any event, a United States Citizen, and entitled to an education, which won't start until a vaccination checklist as long as your arm has been delivered.

That creates a pool of immunity that, if deep enough with respect to the population, makes a whole range of diseases things of the past. That may not be completely true of our newly legal millions of immigrants under a Compact of Free Association.

What the negotiators must do is establish agreement that the vaccines will be provided and the costs will be split. Ideally it would be tied to the passport process, so no I-94 permit would be issued without either a solid record of vaccinations or on-the-spot provision. Of course, that still leaves the Mexicans who are here now and would apply for their Mexican passport at the local U.S.

post office, but the United States vacci-
nated its entire population against polio,
and annually administers millions of
flue shots. Handling 12 million folks
with some vaccination gaps ought not to
be insurmountable.

Besides, the negotiators ought to
ponder that if an almost-2,000-mile
border is porous to people, it is transparent to microbes, which don't check
nationality before getting to their often
deadly work.

Starting date and term

If the recent impasse of immigration
in the United States Congress and the
wide social gulf displayed in the Mexican
presidential election in 2006 are any in-
dicators, this is an issue to either be addressed soon or to carry as a burden for
the next 20 years. Negotiations between
sovereign nations can drag on for years
upon years, in part because those doing
the negotiating have no particular interest in seeking other employment and in
part because one of the easiest answers

200

for an elected leader to give to any impertinent question is "That's in negotiations."

Here, ain't none of us got that kind of time. Mexico can't afford to lose either the social outlet or revenue that immigration generates and the United States can't afford to lose the labor. When the Mayor of the City of New York, a political entity one-third bigger than Israel, testifies that the economy would tank if it weren't for that labor, it's probably worth a listen.

And that listening should involve both Mexico and the United States. And after listening, it's not only worth action, it requires action both for the self interest of each of these magnificent nations and for the principles that surpass nationhood, the ones that say human beings worth the name help each other.

So if it takes 280-odd pages to hammer together a Compact of Free Association between the United States and nations of islands in the Pacific, can we expect a stack of paper the size of the Empire State Building when the compact is between Mexico and the United States? Yes, if we let the lawyers, nit-harvesters and rules-for-everything crowd off leash, no if we keep hammering that this would be a document of basic principles.

That means the distinguished negotiators would agree on a document that said "Holders of valid Mexican passports who meet other basic qualifications for entry to the United States shall be admitted and may live, work and study without limitation, but shall not pursue U.S. citizenship except through already established means and must comply with both the laws of the United States of America and the United States of Mexico."

Bureaucrats from both sides will want to add *"but in no case shall this be permitted unless said Holders (for which see Definition Part A3/Subsection2) provide satisfactory evidence that on the third Tuesday of months with the letter "R" in the English spelling of said months, each Holder is able to hop on said person's left foot, while holding their nose with their right hand and whistling The Star Spangled Banner in three separate musical keys."*

But maybe we should let them add stuff like that—on a jointly administered island someplace, where they can do no more harm and have liberal family visitation rights.

The term of the document should cover ten years from the date of implementation, which should not lag the date of signing by more than one year. Ten years of actual experience making this work will tell both Mexico and the United States what needs tweaking, what works just fine, what new things have developed and how long the next term should be.

The document should have no provisions on changing its terms except through negotiation between two sovereign nations. This isn't a constitution, nor is it just a trade deal, but great care must be taken to avoid making it more than it is or less than it must be. If it works right, it will be NAFTA as it should have been for us and our southern neighbors.

The document should scrupulously avoid hot-button issues like a unified currency, legal or social conformity. We're not talking about a United States of North America, and if we were, our Canadian friends would feel left out, to say the least. We're talking about a way to rationalize and humanize an existing condition that has developed between two nations and is a problem for both.

If the leaders of both Mexico and the United States manage to get this idea moving, the benefits deserve restating.

Mexico gets an outlet for the discontents of its existing poor population, helping it to continue its rise to a free, democratic and capitalistic society in the first rank of nations. But that goal will take time and support and this is what a Compact of Free Association would buy.

The United States gets the labor it needs, and all the economic pluses that labor's spending will generate, and gets itself out of the shameful betrayal of its founding principles. We have been say-

204

ing "...all men are created equal and that they are endowed by their Creator with certain unalienable rights...except, of course you folks," for far too long.

Paradoxically, opening our arms by giving the labor that we need a way to come and work here legally should increase the control of the border. If there were a way for a jornalero and his family to come here in an air-conditioned bus, instead of via coyote transport in a sweltering 18-wheel death trap or a long and deadly hike through a forbidding desert, guess which form of transport would be out of business?

And if, for some reason, an illegal from South America somehow crosses the now-already-pretty tight Mexican southern border, how nice it would be if the first thing they faced on an attempt to cross Mexico's northern border illegally were Mexican Federales, not the U.S. National Guard.

These are possibilities, not fantasies, and they can be made realities, but that must not put down its deepest roots at the national level, but at the individual level. Every human being, whether in the United States or Mexico, has a life.

How they conduct that life, what they believe in and support and oppose is how that life—their watch—will be judged if there is a judgment or remembered if there is not. For this idea of a Compact of Free Association to work, every adult in both Mexico and the United States must look at the current situation, with all its horrors and abuses and denials of what the constitutions of both great nations say are basic human rights.

And then they must stand and say: "Not on my watch!"

They must say it to each other, to their neighbors, to their elected leaders, to anyone who will listen. They must continue to say it until something different starts to happen. Because what is happening now about illegal immigration is a shame and a sorrow, to which we must all say "Not on my watch!"

"My watch" is the duty of every human being to advance and defend humanity, especially when it is under at-

206

tack. We all got the duty when we took our first breath and we will only relinquish it with our last.

Right now, humanity and basic freedoms are under attack on the border between Mexico and the United States, and for citizens of both these neighbors, a reminder:

It is our watch and our shared duty calls, but it is up to each of us, individually, to take a stand and say:

Not on my watch!

Endnotes

---

[i] Lincoln, probably 1846, 1847; Library of Congress, attributed to Nicholas H. Shephard

[ii] CIA World Factbook

[iii] Public Domain, Wikipedia

[iv] Spelling changed to conform with American English

[v] Unattributed stamp photo from web.

[vi] For the record, the author's son, Andrew L. Blasko, works at the Heritage Foundation.

[vii] Copyright 2006 Heritage Foundation; used with permission and thanks.

[viii] Source: Office of the Mayor at nyc.gov.